THE WINNER'S GUIDE TO
Optimist
SAILING

VIDEOS BY GARY JOBSON

The Volvo Ocean Race: The Official Video of the Volvo Ocean Race

Caution to the Wind: 1997/98 Whitbread Round the World Race

Bonanza in Savannah (1996 Yachting Olympics)

Expedition Antarctica

1995 America's Cup: Higher & Faster

1993/94 Whitbread Round the World Race

A Portrait of Cape Horn: The Beauty and the Fury

Whitbread: The First 20 Years

With Swelling Sails: The New York Yacht Club's Sesquicentennial Celebration (narration with Walter Cronkite)

1992 America's Cup

Sailing Quarterly Video Magazine (24 one-hour volumes produced from 1989 to 1995)

Best of Grand Prix Sailing

1989/90 Whitbread Round the World Race

1988 America's Cup

BOOKS BY GARY JOBSON

Gary Jobson's Championship Sailing: The Definitive Guide for Skippers, Tacticians, and Crew

Fighting Finish: The Volvo Ocean Race Round the World, 2001–2002

An America's Cup Treasury: The Lost Levick Photographs, 1893–1937

Sailing Fundamentals: The Official Learn-to-Sail Manual of the American Sailing Association and the United States Coast Guard Auxiliary, revised and updated

Championship Tactics: How Anyone Can Sail Faster, Smarter, and Win Races, with Tom Whidden and Adam Loory

World Class Sailing, with Martin Luray

Speed Sailing, with Mike Toppa

Storm Sailing

Gary Jobson's How to Sail

The Racing Edge, with Ted Turner

U.S.Y.R.U. Sailing Instructor's Manual

The Yachtsman's Pocket Almanac, revised

THE WINNER'S GUIDE TO

Optimist
SAILING

Gary Jobson *and* Jay Kehoe

Illustrations by Brad Dellenbaugh
Photographs by Dan Nerney

International Marine / McGraw-Hill

Camden, Maine • New York • Chicago • San Francisco •
Lisbon • London • Madrid • Mexico City • Milan • New Delhi
• San Juan • Seoul • Singapore • Sydney • Toronto

FOR

ASHLEIGH

AND

BROOKE

The McGraw·Hill Companies

2 3 4 5 6 7 8 9 0 DOC DOC 0 9 8 7

© 1997, 2004 by Jobson Sailing, Inc.

This edition published 2004 by International Marine, a division of The McGraw-Hill Companies.

First published in the United States by Simon & Schuster Inc.

Library of Congress Cataloging-in-Publication Data
Jobson, Gary.
   The winner's guide to optimist sailing / by Gary Jobson and Jay Kehoe ; illustrations by Brad Dellenbaugh ; photographs by Dan Nerney.
     p.   cm.
   Originally published: New York : Simon & Schuster, c1997.
   Includes index.
   ISBN 0-07-143467-4 (alk. paper)
   1. Boating for children. 2. Yacht racing. I. Kehoe, Jay. II. Title.
   GV777.56.J63 1997
   797.124—dc22   2003069166

Questions regarding the ordering of this book should be addressed to
The McGraw-Hill Companies
Customer Service Department
P.O. Box 547
Blacklick, OH 43004
Retail customers: 1-800-262-4729
Bookstores: 1-800-722-4726

Photographs by Dan Nerney. Photo on page ii by Onne van der Wal.
Illustrations by Brad Dellenbaugh.

Contents

Introduction

In twenty-five years of working with youth sailing programs across the country I've seen it happen hundreds of times, but it still brings tears of joy to my eyes. There is no greater elation than watching a child's nervousness dissolve into a triumphant smile as the skipper leaves the dock alone in a small sailboat and successfully returns to shore.

The International Optimist Dinghy Class has seen explosive growth and unequaled popularity in the United States. I am excited to see *The Winner's Guide to Optimist Sailing* available to young skippers, their parents, and their instructors. The authors have done an excellent job providing the most current Optimist-specific information while incorporating the excellent teaching techniques developed by the U.S. Sailing Training Program.

The International Optimist Dinghy Class has emerged as the boat of choice for the majority of youth sailing programs in the United States and around the world. Sailed around the globe by children through age fifteen, it is an excellent way to learn to sail craft while providing competition at numerous local, regional, national, and international regattas. The opportunities to enjoy sailing, travel, and making friends all over the world are unequaled by any other youth boat. The Optimist is a simple, safe boat that a young child can learn to sail and quickly experience self-confidence and success.

Gary Jobson, who is also a father of three young sailors, is world renowned for his successes on the water, his skills as a teacher, and his contributions to the sport of sailing. *The Winner's Guide to Optimist Sailing* brings a crucial link to the learn-to-sail process by emphasizing the importance of having a perfect youth boat, a national instructor training program, and now an Optimist-specific book to complement a sailing program's curriculum.

Coauthor Jay Kehoe has been a strong force in the growth of the Optimist in the USA. He coaches all levels of Optimist sailing, from the young beginner to the world championship team members.

This book will serve you well as the boat-specific curriculum for your Optimist sailor. Use it as you incorporate the training standards set by your national authority.

JONI PALMER
Executive Director
U.S. Optimist Dinghy Association

Welcome to Optimist Sailing

Optimist Fun

Sailing is a sport that will last for a lifetime. You can choose your own skill level, ranging from simple pleasure sailing all the way up to intense Olympic or America's Cup competition.

It all starts with the Optimist dinghy. As you master the techniques of Optimist dinghy sailing, you will develop skills that apply to boats of all sizes. And while the Optimist dinghy is the perfect training boat for beginning sailors, there is also stiff competition within the class.

The world's best sailors all got their start sailing small boats. Small boats put you closer to the wind and the water, and their effects on a small boat are immediate. Unlike larger boats, everything happens instantly in a dinghy. As you sail your Optimist, you will learn to use your body weight, sail trim, and steering abilities in harmony with the wind and water. You will see the results, and just as quickly find out what other sailors know: sailing is a joy.

The fundamentals of sailing are easy to learn. In a few short days, using this book as a guide, you will be sailing efficiently on all points of sailing.

After learning the basics, plan to keep developing these skills. It takes time and practice to become proficient at anything. Concert pianists do not quit when they know the scales. They refine, and practice, and study, and practice, and learn, and practice. The same is true in sailing.

The keys to excelling at any activity are mastering basic skills, practicing them, and recognizing the pleasure this brings.

Today, many sailors are lucky to have sailing instructors or coaches to help make the process easy and fun. Be patient. Keep trying. Ask questions. There are no shortcuts. Everyone has to follow the same learning path.

And it's a learning path that many have followed, from sailing legends like Paul Elvstrom and Buddy Melges to Albert Einstein, the brilliant physicist.

The brilliant physicist Albert Einstein loved sailing and spent time sailing on the water in his youth.

Yes, Albert Einstein. He loved sailing. He was delighted by the way the wind moved the boat through the water, by the way it sounded, the way it felt. But he had to learn how to sail, just like you, and he had to practice too, to make his boat sail as best it could. That is part of the joy of sailing, after all.

As time goes by, Optimist sailing can open up broad horizons. You are joining more than three hundred thousand Optimist sailors from more than eighty-five countries worldwide by sailing and competing in an Optimist dinghy.

The Optimist class is even in the *Guinness Book of World Records* for having the biggest regatta ever: 456 Optimist dinghies competed at Lake Garda, Italy.

There are many sailors who learned in an Optimist, and who get the most pleasure out of their local club's races, or a good sail on a nice day. And there are some who have gone on to win Olympic medals, world championships in other classes, the Whitbread Round-the-World Race, and the America's Cup. You too could be a champion in the near future. Make this book a special friend, and it will be a lasting one.

How the Optimist Came to Be

At first glance, the International Optimist Dinghy looks a little unusual. The hull has a rectangular appearance. It might remind you of a floating soapbox derby car. And you would be close to guessing its origins.

In 1948, a group of people in Clearwater, Florida, who belonged to the Optimists International organization noticed that a lot of young people—and their parents—were fascinated by soapbox derby cars. Since Clearwater is bordered by Clearwater Bay and the Gulf of Mexico, these men asked boat designer Clark Mills to come up with a boat that would get the young people on the water, just as the soapbox derby cars were getting them on the roads.

The idea was to design a boat that was sturdy, stable, easy to build and maintain, and that also sailed well. Clark Mills designed a boat that could be built by a parent and child in a garage, using one sheet of plywood, glue, and screws. It had a simple rig, and it was a good boat for the youngest children to learn in, but it sailed well enough to provide good competition for the older sailors as they perfected their sailing and racing skills. Thus was born the Optimist pram (as they called sailing dinghies in those days), the perfect boat for kids ages eight to fifteen. It became a favorite in the Tampa Bay area. In 1954 Axel Damgaard, the skipper of a Danish tall ship visiting the United States, saw the prams and took the idea home to Denmark. He started a campaign to make the boat popular throughout Scandinavia, and it worked!

As the boat gained popularity, a way had to be found to make sure the boat stayed basically the same for all sailors in all countries to ensure fair competition. Measurement and design rules were put into effect so that there would be equal competition as a one-design class.

The Optimist pram had morphed into the International Optimist Dinghy, or IOD. When it gained even more popularity in Europe during the 1960s, the International Optimist Dinghy Association was organized, and by the end of the 1970s, the boat had won the hearts of young sailors in South America, Africa, and Asia as well.

This boat is a truly international class, and there are important regattas literally all over the world for young competitors. In 1995, there were over four hundred regattas for Optimists in the United States alone.

Presently there are seventy-nine member countries of the International Optimist Dinghy Association. Among the top sailors in the United States who grew up sailing Optimist dinghies are Ed Baird, a top match-racing sailor and former Laser World champion; Allison Jolly, Olympic gold medalist in the 470 Class in 1988; and Morgan Reeser, silver medalist in the Men's 470 Class in 1992.

There are several reasons for this little boat's huge popularity. It really does sail. It really is easy to maintain. While you can still build a sailing dinghy out of a sheet of plywood, and while the boats are still used to very good advantage in many junior sailing programs, the IOD in its modern form is a very controlled one-design. This limits the role money plays in a competitor's bag of tricks. Boat-handling ability, tactical prowess, and basic sailing skills are what matter in the Optimist class, not expensive add-ons and constant upgrades.

Many young people do learn to sail, and then to race, in an Optimist. But the boat is not limited to basics, as any Optimist regatta will prove. The competition is stiff, and when the good sailors "age out" (the year they turn sixteen), they take the skills they have learned on to other classes of boats.

Whether you choose pleasure sailing or competition as your goal, no boat will give you a better start than an Optimist.

Getting
Started

The Boat and Equipment

Parts of the Boat

The parts of a boat have traditional, nautical names. Some you may know already, and some may seem pretty odd. But it's easy to learn them, once you know what—and where—they are.

When you think about your boat, try to think about the names for the different parts. Soon you will be speaking the language of the sea.

HULL

The boat itself is called the **hull.** It sits in the water, and you sit in it.

The front of the hull is called the **bow.** This rhymes with "cow." But you wouldn't want a cow on your bow.

It would be very difficult to sail an Optimist dinghy with a cow on your boat.

A completely rigged Optimist ready to sail.

The back of the hull is called the **stern.** The flat back part of the stern is called the **transom.**

As you face the bow from inside the boat, the right side is the **starboard** side, and the left side is the **port** side. On the water, you say starboard instead of right, and port instead of left.

At the bow there is a flat board that connects the hull. This is the **mast thwart,**

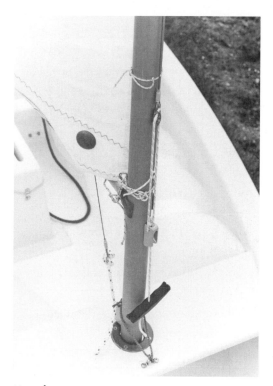

Mast thwart

Be sure your bag has the correct air pressure.

sometimes known as a mast partner. The purpose is to hold the mast and to give the boat strength in the bow area.

Right underneath the hole in the mast thwart is the **mast step.**

Moving toward the stern, in the center of the boat, you find the **daggerboard trunk.**

Just **aft** of (behind) the daggerboard trunk is a low wall called a **bulkhead.**

On the insides of the hull on some boats there are two compartments. These hold air bags. Some boats have air bags without covering compartments. These air bags are your **flotation.** If your boat

tips over (**capsizes**), the air bags make sure it does not sink.

There is another air bag that goes across the inside of the transom. It is not in a compartment. The air bags might seem like good pillows. They are *not*. They burst. It is a very bad idea to sit, jump, or lie on the air bags. Take care of your air bags with the proper amount of inflation.

The top edges of the sides of your boat are called the **gunwales** or rails (say "gunnels" and you'll sound like an old salt). Sometimes you will need to sit on the gunwale either to keep your boat flat in the water or to tip it on purpose. That is called **sitting on the rail,** or "hiking out."

When you are out on the rail, you will tuck your feet under the **hiking straps** to help you keep your balance and allow you to lean way out. These are attached under the transom air bag and lead forward on each side of the deck until they attach to the bulkhead.

On the inside, the overhang of the gunwale is called the **coaming.** You can coil up your **painter** (bowline) and tuck it under the coaming of the bow to keep it out of the way.

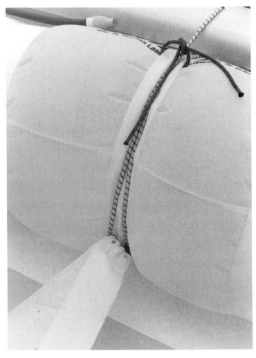

Use bungee cord to hold in your air bag and also lift your hiking strap.

SAIL

Your sail is a **sprit rig.** It is not the usual triangle shape (called a **Marconi rig**). The sprit rig sail looks as if the tip at the top of the triangle has been cut off at an angle, lower in front than in back.

The front edge of the sail is called the **luff.**

The back edge of the sail is called the **leech.**

The top forward edge is called the **head.**

The bottom edge of the sail is called the **foot.**

The top front corner of the sail is called the **throat.**

The bottom front corner of your sail is called the **tack.**

The bottom back corner is called the **clew.**

The top back corner of your sail is called the **peak.**

Along the leech, there are two little sleeves sewn into your sail. They are called **batten pockets.** The **battens** slide inside them to keep the leech from curling.

Along the luff and foot, and at the corners of your sail, are the **grommets,** holes with metal reinforcements. You tie your sail onto the spars through these holes.

There are practice sails and also racing sails that come in different weights and materials. You choose the kind you need depending on your skill level and weight.

Each part of the sail has a name. These parts are the same for all sails, no matter what size the boat.

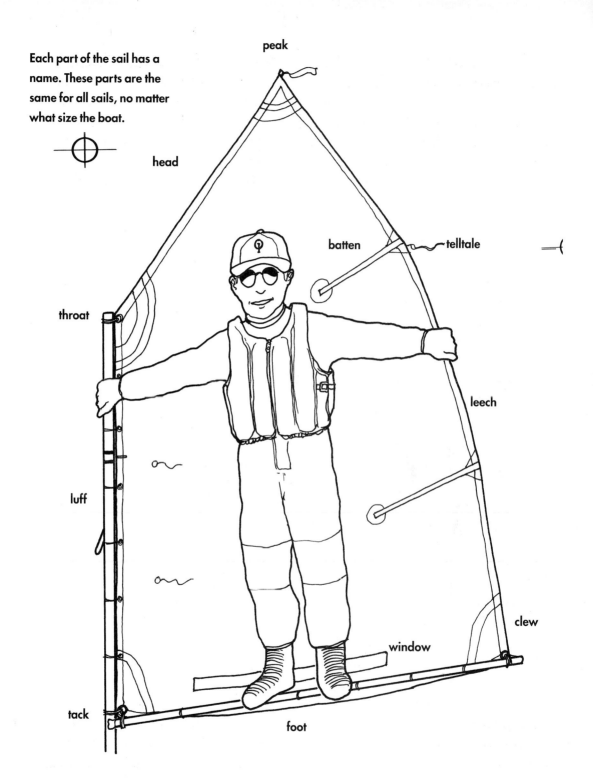

peak

head

batten

telltale

throat

leech

luff

clew

window

tack

foot

Parts of a Boat

1. hull
2. bow
3. stern
4. transom
5. starboard
6. port
7. mast thwart
8. mast step
9. daggerboard trunk
10. bulkhead
11. flotation
12. gunwale
13. luff
14. leech
15. foot
16. head
17. tack
18. clew
19. throat
20. peak
21. batten
22. grommets
23. mast
24. boom
25. boom jaws
26. sprit
27. wind indicator
28. hiking strap
29. daggerboard
30. rudder
31. tiller
32. tiller extension
33. mainsheet
34. shackle
35. sail tie
36. outhaul
37. boom vang

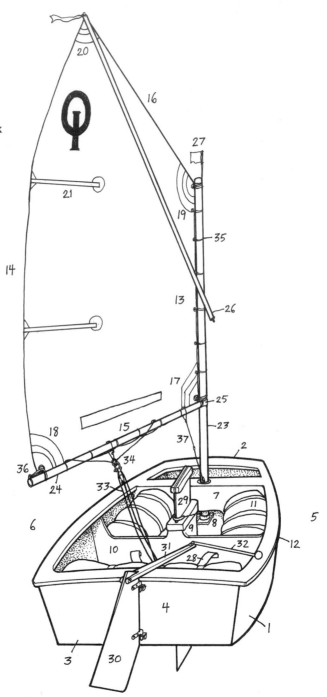

SPARS

The Optimist has three **spars.**

The **mast** is the fattest. It has to hold the sail up.

The **boom** fits along the bottom of the sail and holds the sail down. It is attached to the mast with the fitting called the **boom jaws.** These are made of plastic and held on by tensioning the sail ties.

The **sprit** angles up from about halfway up the mast to the peak of the sail, and gives the sail its shape.

Without the mast, boom, and sprit, your sail would look just like a sheet hung out to dry with only one clothespin.

All spars are made out of aluminum. The club rig spars are made out of a strong, heavy-duty aluminum. The racing spars are made out of a stiffer anodized aluminum.

There are **measurement bands** taped onto your mast and boom: two bands on the mast and one band on the sail. These indicate the legal limits of where your sail can be fastened. You must keep the measurement band on your sail within these bands. This will also help preserve the sail's proper shape.

At the top of the mast, there can be a **wind indicator,** also called a **masthead fly.**

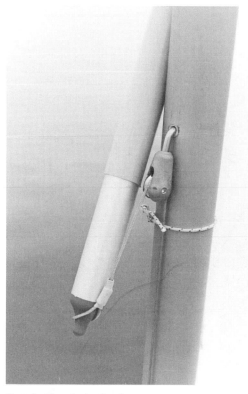

Standard sprit rig that is most commonly used throughout the world.

BLADES

To keep the boat from sliding across the top of the water like a leaf blown by the wind across a puddle, an Optimist has **blades.**

One *blade* is called a **daggerboard.** It slides into the daggerboard trunk. You can put it all the way down, or you can take it all the way out, just the way a dagger fits into its sheath.

Daggerboards have a front, or **leading edge,** which is rounded, and a back, or **trailing edge,** which is sharp.

The daggerboard must have a tie attached to it so it cannot fall out of the boat. And the daggerboard trunk has bungee cords on it to hold the daggerboard in any position you like.

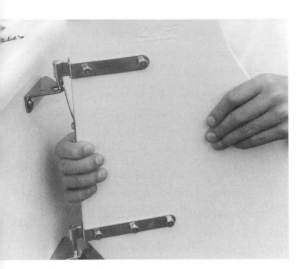

Pintles and gudgeons

The other blade is the **rudder.** It allows you to steer the boat. The rudder hangs off the transom into the water. It is attached to the transom with **gudgeons** on the boat and **pintles** on the rudder and should have a swivel keeper "rudder lock" to make sure it stays in place.

Attached to the top of the rudder is the **tiller.** It reaches into the boat so you don't have to hang over the stern to move the rudder.

And at the other end of the tiller is the **tiller extension** or **hiking stick.** This lets you move the tiller even if you are farther away from it than your arm will reach. You can steer sitting on the rail by using your hiking stick. There are many opinions on the best way to hold the hiking stick. Some sailors will hold it like a microphone. In this case think of the hiking stick as an extension to your arm. Many sailors prefer to hold the hiking stick across the chest.

The proper way to hold the hiking stick is across your chest like a microphone. Keeping the hiking stick low gives you better control of your rudder.

Do not hold the hiking stick at its base or you will oversteer.

We find it better to keep the hiking stick low so that every action of your wrist goes directly to your rudder. This prevents you from oversteering.

Lines and Equipment

All ropes on a boat are called **lines.** Even what you might think of as overgrown string is called a line.

Moving from bow to stern, the first line on your boat is called the **painter** or **bowline.** Usually, the painter fits through a hole in the bow and ties (very securely!) to your mast step.

It must be the sort of line that floats. It must be at least eight meters long (approximately twenty-five feet).

This is the line that you will use to tie up to the dock, or to attach to another boat (a tow boat, for example).

Your **mainsheet** is the line that lets you pull your sail in, or let your sail out. The mainsheet is led through a series of blocks (pulleys) known as "parts." These blocks give you a mechanical advantage when you try to pull in the sail on a windy day. This mainsheet attachment is called the **mainsheet bridle.**

The mainsheet parts attach to the boom with a **snap shackle** or **snap hook.** This holds the mainsheet secure, but makes it very easy to undo if you need to get it off in a hurry. Make sure it does not open too easily, or it can catch on your PFD (personal flotation device) or something else. Knots will also work.

Your sail is tied on with a couple different types of **sail ties.** First, there are the long ones for the tack, clew, and head. These are usually made out of very strong line called "prestretched" line that has been treated to minimize stretching. Spectra and Kevlar are common types of thread used to weave this kind of line.

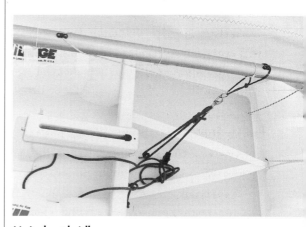

Mainsheet bridle

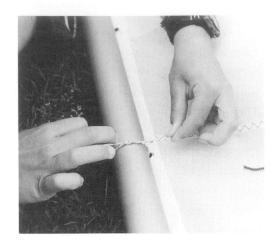

These lines are attached to the stress points of your sail. The lines need to be long enough to tie around the spar.

Sail ties need to be the following length and diameter:

1. Halyard   Spectra/Kevlar 45 cm/4 mm
2. Halyard brake Spectra/Kevlar 45 cm/4 mm
3. Sail ties (mast) Spectra/Kevlar 40 cm/2 mm
4. Sail ties (boom) Spectra/Kevlar 25 cm/2 mm
5. Tack sail ties   Spectra/Kevlar 45 cm/4 mm
6. Clew sail ties   Spectra/Kevlar 40 cm/4 mm

Sail ties along the mast should be wrapped twice around and tied so the sail sits along the mast. Boom ties should be 1 cm loose so the sail can flop over the boom when tacking.

The tack needs to be tied with two thick ties to the mast and boom separately. They should be tight, without space between the spar and the sail.

At the head of the sail, you will have a **top-sail tie** or **halyard tie.** This line holds your sail up.

Mast and boom sail ties should be done with care.

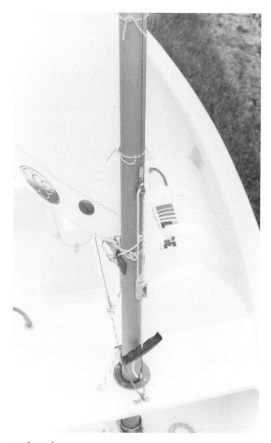

Halyard preventer

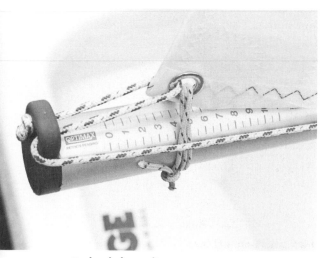

Outhaul-clew adjustment

You will also have a **halyard preventer.** This ties around your mast through an eyestrap, which is a little lower than your halyard. This prevents the halyard sail tie from lifting right up and off the mast.

The tension on the **sprit** is an important adjustment for shaping the sail. The lower end of the sprit is attached to a sprit adjuster, sometimes called the sprit halyard. A small loop or wire is pushed through a small protruding knob at the bottom of the sprit. This line (or wire) is passed through a block attached to the mast about six inches up from the end of the sprit.

The line continues through a cam cleat in front of the mast at the gooseneck. We recommend a 2-to-1 sprit adjustment system. For quick adjustments it helps to attach a handle to the end of this line after it passes through the cam cleat.

Your **outhaul** is a line that does what it says: it hauls the sail out through a fitting on the aft end of your boom. It starts at the fitting with a stopper knot at the end, threads through the clew grommet, and back through the fitting, then along the boom to a cleat. You should be able to adjust this line depending on the wind conditions.

The clew needs one thick sail tie wrapped twice and not obstructing the outhaul line.

You also have a **boom vang.** This can be a combination of wire and line or simply line. It keeps the boom from

Boom vang, and boom preventer tack attachments

flying up in a breeze. The vang wire loops over the boom (a preventer knob on the top of the boom prevents the vang from sliding forward), attaches to a line, and the line is fed through a cleat on the mast right above the mast thwart.

At the boom jaws, there is a **boom preventer.** This line runs from the boom jaws to twist around a fitting on the mast, and adds another sail-shaping control, as well as making sure your sail stays within the measurement bands.

Other lines to remember are those that connect various pieces of equipment or parts of your boat to the hull.

They include the **mast tie** line. This makes sure your mast does not lift out of the mast step. This is very important and must be tied tightly. If your mast lifts part of the way out of the boat when you tip over, the weight of the water on the sail could cause the mast to crack the mast thwart. You could also lose the mast entirely.

The line that is tied to your daggerboard makes sure that it can't fall out or drift away from your boat. And the same goes for the lines tied to your bailers.

Keeping your lines in good shape, and making sure that they are correctly rigged and that your knots are correctly tied are important skills to learn.

Have extra lines just in case you need them. You can tuck extra sail ties under the straps that keep your air bag in the transom.

BAILERS

Unless you are sailing on a very quiet day, chances are you will **take on** water. This means a wave hits your boat and washes into it. Water in a boat makes it harder to steer. And of course it adds weight, which will slow you down.

So you need to be able to get the water out. That's called **bailing,** and it's done with a **bailer.**

Bailers are usually plastic containers

Bailing

that are tied onto your boat. You can use anything that will hold water and that you can hold easily. Square plastic iced-tea pitchers work best. When you take on water, bail it out as soon as you can. Tie your bailer in with line or bungee cord

Sailing with water in your boat is slow. Try to bail the water out.

through the coaming or tie it to your centerboard retaining shock cord.

Also take a sponge, so you can get *all* the water out. You'll need a sponge to make sure your boat is dry when you put it away. A sponge also helps to keep the boat clean.

LIFE JACKETS

No matter how well you swim, you must wear a **life jacket.** It's a rule. Life jackets (also called **personal flotation devices,** or **PFDs**) will keep you floating while you are in the water, and let you concentrate on other things besides keeping your head above the water.

Pick out a life jacket that is comfortable for you. You want to be able to move easily in your life jacket. Jump around in it. Crawl around in it. Twist around in it.

Make sure it fits properly. Always wear the correct size. Too small and you sink. Too big, and it will float off without you. Sit down in it. If it raises your arms or comes up around your ears, it's too big, and will be uncomfortable when you sit in your boat.

Have someone try to pull it off over your head. If it comes off this way, it's still too big.

Life jackets come in all sorts of great colors, and since you have to wear one every time you go for a sail, pick out one you like. Bright colors are recommended so you can easily be seen if you fall

A life jacket should fit securely. To test it, be sure someone can't pull it over your head.

overboard. Remember, life jackets also add a layer of warmth on those chilly sailing days. Put your name on the outside of your life jacket with an indelible marker.

Another important safety device every Opti sailor should have is a **whistle.** This will let you get the attention of another boat if you need help in the water. Whistles are tied right to your life jacket,

so they are handy but out of your way. Do not tie them or hang them around your neck.

Don't go tooting your whistle just for the fun of it. Remember what happened to the boy who cried "wolf"?

CLOTHING

Be smart about what you wear sailing. Dress sensibly for comfort and for the weather. There is a big choice of sailing clothing, so you should be able to pick out things you like, and that also make sense to wear. You want to be able to move as freely and easily as possible. Some of the trendy sailing clothing is very sensible, too!

All dressed and ready to go! You lose body heat very quickly through your head, so be sure to wear a warm hat in chilly weather.

Warm weather sailing gear:
life jacket, hiking pants, and
dinghy boots (with socks).

Hats are very important. You will need one for hot, sunny days. Tie it to you or to your life jacket. Experienced sailors always have their hats secured with a piece of line. You will look like a pro, and lose fewer hats this way.

A winter or cold-weather hat is just as important. People lose 90 percent of their body heat from the tops of their heads, so cover yours up and stay warmer. Ear flaps are great, and hats with ear flaps now come in all colors—and some interesting shapes, too.

The main thing to remember about dressing for sailing is that you want to stay comfortable in whatever the weather happens to be. Sailors tend to have more different kinds of clothing than any other kind of sporting enthusiasts. Your new bathing suit may be super-looking, but it's not going to keep you warm and dry on a day that is cold and rainy. And some of the best sailing is on cold, rainy days.

Only wear sea boots that you can take off easily. You don't want your boots to fill up with water. Choose dinghy boots, reef walkers, or wet suit booties if you need that sort of protection. Personally we like

Even when it's cold and
windy, you can still get
sunburn! Use sun cream.

Dry suits are very popular in cold weather.

Quick list:

No bare feet!

Wear at least a T-shirt to keep the sun off.

Apply sunscreen frequently.

Sunglasses are a must.

Hats against hot sun and cold wind.

Always wear a PFD.

FOUL WEATHER GEAR

There are wet suits and dry suits, heavy-weather flotation suits, slickers, boots, jackets, all sorts of foul weather gear. Choose pieces that make sense for the sailing conditions you will be experiencing.

to wear socks with docksiders or dinghy boots.

The fact is, you will sail better with the proper clothing. It just makes sense. If you are comfortably dressed for the weather and for adequate movement, you will not be thinking about the fact that your wet bathing suit is too chilly and chafing, and you will be better able to concentrate on the sailing.

Safety

Safety on the water is really just a matter of using your head. Don't go out for a sail in winds that are too strong for you to be able to control your boat. Don't set sail if you can see lightning anywhere on the horizon! Have someone ashore watching out for you, or better yet, in a safety boat on the water. As a rule you should always sail with a partner in another boat.

Before you set sail, check the weather forecast. Know where the wind is coming from. Will it blow you and your boat away from the shore, or back toward it? Is the current strong? Which way will it pull your boat? Answer these questions before you launch.

On board, safety is also a matter of using common sense. Remember to wear your life jacket. Have a whistle attached to it. Check the gear before you go out so you know it's all in safe condition. Make sure the bailers and daggerboard are tied into the boat. Make sure the mast tie line is secure.

Make sure the boom bridle can stretch (under pressure) absolutely no lower than 10 cm from the boom. You do not want to have a deep triangle here. It can catch you or your life jacket as you tack. A distance of 5 cm is recommended.

Check your air bags. They must be inflated, but not overinflated. As the day warms up, the air in them will expand and could cause them to pop. They should have enough air in them so that they give when you press your finger into them.

Take a short paddle or a paddle that will tuck in behind your air bag.

Keep all your gear close to your daggerboard to center the weight in the boat.

Check your knots. Everything tight?

On the water, know the basic Rules of the Road and obey them.

Wear sunblock and a hat if the sun is out. Sun reflecting off the water can give you a painful burn a lot sooner than in your backyard. Always take along a water bottle. And sunglasses really are necessary. Polarized ones are the best.

If you feel too cold, wet, hot, or tired, sail in immediately. Be smart. Learn your limits. Four hours is a long time to spend in a boat. Save enough energy to put your boat away properly. You want to have a good time on the water, not push yourself beyond the limits of the weather or your abilities.

If you pay attention to basic safety rules, then you will have more confidence in your sailing, and enjoy it more. And that's what sailing is all about!

Boating Etiquette

Yes, there is something called *boating etiquette.* And just like safety afloat, it is a matter of using your head, combined with plain old good manners.

Knowing the basic Rules of the Road on the water is important, especially when there are lots of other boats out. Knowing what is expected of you, and what to expect from other boats, makes being on the water more fun and safer.

Because the Optimist is smaller than most boats, you can really zip around in one. But don't try any small-space maneuvers until you are absolutely confident that you can control your boat. Sailing in and out of moored boats can be fun, but hitting mooring lines—or the boats—is not fun for anyone.

Make sure your boat is securely tied at the dock. You wouldn't want another boat to smash into yours, or your boat to smash into the dock. Be courteous here. Knowing how to tie your boat up properly means you won't be taking up space meant for the *Queen Mary.* Or the commodore of the yacht club.

Be thoughtful. If someone needs a helping hand, be sure to offer yours. This pays off. When you need help, you're sure to get it if you have been willing to help others.

Be considerate. You may have the right-of-way, but if the other boat has obvious reason not to change course, don't force the issue just to cause a wreck. The whole idea of sailing rules is to *prevent* collisions, not to assign blame.

Be aware. Learn from more experienced sailors.

Be persistent to get the help you need, but don't cause a fuss at the sailing center. It's no fun for anyone to teach an uncooperative student. Ask until you understand what you want to know, but always be polite.

Knots for Optimists

Optimist sailors need to know how to tie certain knots for certain purposes. Practice until you can tie all of them.

Square Knot
Mast tie in. Fastening sail ties.
Square Knot with Keeper
Securing sail ties.
Bowline
Tying fixed loops. Use at the end of a bowline, mainsheet, tying the bailer of the daggerboard to the boat.
Clove Hitch
Tying up to pilings.
One-Design Knot
Outhaul stopper.
Tying to a Cleat
Tying the painter to a cleat on a dock.
Stopper Knot
Used at the end of the mainsheet.

Knots must be tied properly. There is an old expression, "If you can't tie good knots, tie plenty of them."

figure 8

stopper

square knot

add a keeper knot

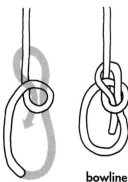

bowline

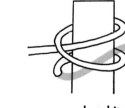

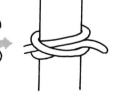

clove hitch around post

tying to a cleat

Transporting Your Optimist Dinghy

Traveling with an Optimist is half the fun of sailing one. There are Optimist regattas all over the country, and in countries all over the world.

Getting the Optimist from one place to another is easy, because it is so small and lightweight. An Optimist can be turned on its deck and tied to the roof of most cars. They can be stacked and towed on a trailer. Most station wagons can hold an Optimist with the back open.

The most important thing is to make sure the boat is tied down securely. Wide webbing straps will protect the corners of the boat. Some sort of pad under the boat will prevent chafe and rub on the boat, and the car, too.

Use a hull cover to protect the hull from weather and road grime.

Remove the air bags, bailers, and the mast step. (Some kinds of mast steps cannot be removed.) These can shift around and get lost. Make sure the painter is coiled and secured tightly or take it off for transporting.

Optimists are easy to cartop.

Team Moo super trailer, which holds twelve Optimist dinghies.

Double-deck Optimist trailer.

Rigs and sails travel best in six-inch PVC-pipe tubes. These can be secured to roof racks or bolted onto trailers. You can check them on airplanes, too.

Sails should be left on the boom and removed from the mast.

Before you transport the boat, check to make sure you have all the necessary gear loaded. Use a written checklist.

Checklist

1. **Life jacket**
2. **Blades**
3. **Mainsheet**
4. **Extra sail ties (one complete set)**
5. **Sunscreen**
6. **Sailing gear**
7. **Spars**

Using a dolly to get the boat in and out of the water makes sailing an Optimist something even a small or young sailor can do by him or herself. Use it on a ramp or on the beach. Dollies fold up and can be packed easily in the car, or checked on a plane.

Care of Boat and Rig

To get the most enjoyment out of your boat and sails, they must be properly maintained. Even a small boat like an Optimist benefits from good maintenance. And all the best sailors make it a practice to keep all their gear organized, neat, clean, and in good condition. Spend the small amount of time it takes to take care of your boat, and it will pay big dividends.

Just keeping your boat clean gives you a lot of pride in your equipment and also allows you to easily see if something is broken. Wash your boat down with fresh water when you come back from sailing. Along the coast you will be sailing in saltwater. Salt can damage your boat's finish. This includes your spars and blades. Wipe your hull off, maybe polish it. It doesn't take long. You can get some salt off yourself at the same time.

Check your lines to make sure everything is in good condition. Better to do it now than to have to race around trying to find replacements before your next sail.

Rolling up a sail will lengthen its life.

But roll your sail carefully and never bend it after you have rolled it. Or you can remove the sail from the mast and roll it along the boom. Make *sure* your battens lie straight along the boom when you do this. Or take them out. Don't lose them!

Turn your boat upside down carefully. Don't grind it into the sand or pavement. Rest it on fenders or padded boards rather than directly on the ground. Cover it if possible. Put your name and sail number on your gear and stow it in the proper place so you'll know where everything is the next time you go for a sail.

Your blades need care, too. Don't leave them in the hot sun. Intense heat can warp your daggerboard, and you want the leading and trailing edges of both your blades in smooth condition. Handle them carefully.

Any block or part of rigging that's giving you trouble should be looked at, and replaced if necessary. A failure on the water could mean that you might be practicing sailing without a rudder, or under strange sail-shape conditions when you don't mean to.

Again, remember that the very best sailors take the very best care of their boats. They don't want to have to think about their gear when they are on the water, so they give it enough attention when they are on land.

Let's Go Sailing

How a Boat Sails

Sailboats move across the top of the water, powered by the wind.

Some sailors might want to go in the same direction as the wind is blowing. Their sails will be at right angles to the boat, so the sails will catch as much wind as possible, the way parachutes catch the air.

The pressure of the wind pushes the boat along the top of the water, just like that old leaf blowing across a puddle.

But a sailboat wouldn't be worth much or be much fun if it could only sail **downwind** (with the wind). What makes a sailboat able to move toward the wind (**upwind**)?

The answer is: the blades.

Under the boat, the daggerboard is cutting into the water. If the boat is pointing in a direction other than downwind, when the wind pushes against the sail in one direction, the wide, flat side of the daggerboard is pressed against the water in the other direction. Instead of slipping sideways, the boat is forced ahead. This combination of pressure is the engine that powers a sailboat upwind. The force on a boat is a little like a watermelon seed squeezed between your fingers. The counteracting forces propel the boat forward.

But how is this engine driven? Who decides where the sailboat will go?

The person controlling the rudder (called the **helmsman**) and the sail is steering this engine.

The tiller moves the rudder, remember, and the rudder is another blade in the water. This one lets you steer the boat in almost any direction (see "The Points of Sailing" to find out where you cannot make a sailboat go).

Because the sailboat has power from the pressures of the wind on the sail and the daggerboard against the water (upwind) or power directly from the force of the wind on the "pushing" sail (downwind), when you move the rudder to one side or the other the boat will change direction. Just like steering a bike.

At the same time you steer with the rudder, you must also control your sail to keep it full. This is called **sail trim.** Sometimes you need to let the sail out (**easing the mainsheet**) and sometimes you need to pull your sail in to use the wind best.

When you head the boat closer to the direction the wind is coming from, you are **heading up** or **pointing.** To head farther away from the wind, you **head**

In light wind sit in the middle of your boat facing your sail. This helmsman will adjust sail trim and steering as the wind changes.

This boat is sailing in the "safety position." The wind is blowing from the side and the sail is eased way out.

down or **foot.** If a windshift allows you to head up higher, it's called a **lift.** If a windshift doesn't allow you to head as high, it's called a **header.**

Safety position is when the wind is coming from your beam and your sail is all the way out. When you are in the

safety position, the boom will not hit you in the head and the action of the sail will be away from the boat. Also on this course the boat will not sail backwards.

The Points of Sailing

You can sail in any direction you please, except straight into the wind. But by adjusting your sails, your daggerboard, and your weight in the boat, you will always be able to get back to where you started, even if that place seems to be directly into the wind.

How does this work?

First you need to know what the **points of sail** are called.

If you are sailing as close as possible toward where the wind is coming from, then you are **beating,** or sailing **close hauled** or **hard on the wind.** Every sailor will understand what you mean if you use any one of these terms.

If the wind is right behind you (the wind is astern), then you are **running before the wind,** or sailing downwind.

Anytime you are not on the wind or running and the wind is from the side, you are sailing on a **reach. A close reach** is

The fastest point of sail is a reach: when the wind is coming from the side. When you are heading directly into the wind, your boat will not move.

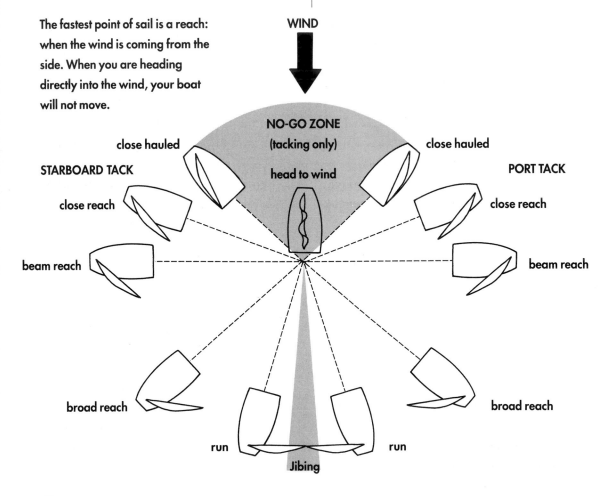

WIND

NO-GO ZONE
(tacking only)

close hauled   close hauled

STARBOARD TACK   head to wind   PORT TACK

close reach   close reach

beam reach   beam reach

broad reach   broad reach

run   run

Jibing

when you are not quite hard on the wind. A **beam reach** is when the wind is coming directly from the side—or the **beam**—of the boat. All boats sail fastest on a beam reach. And a **broad reach** is when you are not quite on a run.

How you adjust your sails for these different points of sail is called your **sail trim.**

If you do end up pointing straight into the wind, you will stop. Your sail will **luff** (shake and flutter). You will lose power, so you won't be able to steer. This is called being **in irons,** or in the **no-go zone.** This is not good and you will end up sailing backwards.

The term "being in irons" comes from the old days of big sailing warships, when sailors were punished by being put in leg irons so they could not move. If a sailing warship got stuck **head-to-wind** (directly facing into the wind), it lost the power to move, and the captain could not steer his boat. So he could not move his boat out of the way of his foe. It was as if the ship had on leg irons and was shackled to one place.

When one of those sailing warships got stuck in irons, it could stay stuck for several hours—plenty of time for the enemy to circle the ship and sink it. The captains did everything possible *not* to get stuck in irons, or in the no-go zone.

No one is going to circle and sink your Optimist, and getting out of irons is much easier for you. It happens sometimes, and

if you know what to do (see "Acceleration, Slowing Down, and Stopping"), you can be on your way quickly.

And the Optimist can also sail backwards. Steering is reversed when you are going in reverse! It's the way to get out of irons, and it looks pretty silly, so it's fun to learn.

Now that you know some of the sailing vocabulary, it's time to get in the boat and go for a sail!

Preparation Before Sailing

Before you launch your boat, make sure you have all your gear. Put it all on the ground near your boat and check it out.

• Check your air bags. They should be full, but not tight. Press on the ones in the flotation compartments and make sure they have air in them. You should be able to press almost to the other side of the air bag with your fingers, but it should take some pressure to do this.

• Make sure the air bag across the transom is full and strapped in securely. Remember, don't overinflate.

• Check your hiking straps. If you use shock cord to keep them up, you can tuck your bailers in behind the triangle the shock cord makes with the daggerboard trunk.

• Never go sailing without telling someone first. We recommend the buddy system. It is always best to have two boats on the water at the same time. And even when you feel comfortable on every point of sail, it's still necessary to make sure someone is on shore keeping an eye out, or better still, to have a friend in a boat on the water who can help if you need it.

• Before you go for a sail, be sure to check out the weather and dress properly. Look at the sky, check out the clouds, listen to the weather forecast, watch the Weather Channel.

• Be sure you have your life preserver on, and don't forget your bailer. Make sure your bailers are tied in with cords long enough to allow you to use them. Also take your whistle and make sure your mast is tied in securely.

• For your first sail, a sunny day with a breeze of about 5 knots is just about perfect for the Optimist.

Rigging

Putting your boat together to go for a sail is called **rigging** your boat.

Rigging your boat for the first time can be pretty interesting. Which part goes where? It's easy once you have done it, so have all your gear ready, get a friend or adult to help, and start rigging.

Put the spars down on the ground in the way they will stand up in the boat.

Lay the sail down over the spars just the way it will fly once you have the boat rigged.

There are two sailing rigs for Optimists. For beginners, the **club rig** is the usual one. It's the one to use if you are just starting to sail an Optimist, or if you are just planning to go for a fun sail (the **racing rig** is described later on in this book).

Rigging your sail is the most important part of rigging your Optimist. Learn how to do it (it's not hard), and then practice until you know exactly where everything belongs.

You should have a mast, a boom, a sprit, a sail, sail ties, a vang, an outhaul, a boom preventer, and your main sheet.

Make sure you can identify all the parts. Name them as you go along. It's easy.

Start by rigging the boom.

Tie the boom preventer onto the boom jaw. This is an important line: it prevents the boom from changing position once you adjust it. Without it, the vang can pull the boom down too much.

If you have a mainsheet bridle, now is the time to rig it. You can leave it rigged after your first sail, checking to make sure it doesn't get too loose.

The bridle has two systems of attachment: pegs and eyestraps. These two fixture points are about 1 meter apart and spread the load of the mainsheet out along the boom so it doesn't bend. We recommend tying a safety line as a bridle preventer about midway along the boom to the mainsheet attachment point. This accomplishes two things: it keeps the mainsheet bridle from stretching down below 10 cm, and if you tighten the line (preventer) up in a big breeze you will bend the boom and depower the leech.

Tie the bridle to the forward peg on the boom. Just forward of the middle of the boom, tie on the ring. Then tie the end of the bridle to the last peg on the boom. You can make a purchase to get this really tight.

The class rule states that the bridle cannot stretch below the 10 cm point. This prevents the bridle from catching your head or other parts of your body and holding them underwater in the event of a capsize.

Another "preventer" is the boom vang. This keeps the angle of the boom from shifting drastically upward. Rig the vang by sliding the wire loop aft of the peg on the boom, or use a bowline knot to tie the line aft of the peg or through the eyestrap on the boom. Feed the other end of the vang line through the cleat on the mast.

Now it's time to start actually tying on the sail.

Start at the clew.

Rig your outhaul first. Be sure to tie a knot (figure-8) in the outhaul line first. Then thread it through the boom end fitting from back to front, through the clew grommet, and back again through the boom end front to back. Take the line down the boom to the cleat, but cleat it loosely.

Then take a clew tie (this should be a stronger, longer piece of line, one that doesn't stretch) and put it through the clew and around the boom twice. If you aren't using longer ties, then tie two sail ties here.

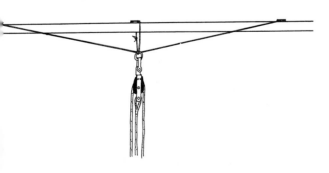

Bridle preventer

Don't tie the sail down too tightly. The foot of the sail should just barely touch the boom here. It should not overlap the boom.

Now tie the rest of the foot of the sail to the boom, working toward the mast end. Use square knots with a single keeper knot. A keeper is an added hitch, to ensure that the knot doesn't untie.

You want to try to have all the sail ties hold the sail the same distance from the boom. Perfect is 5 mm. That's about the width of a pencil. Work very hard to be able to tie your sail on with a consistent separation of sail and boom. This might take practice. And a windy day will show you if your knots are properly tied! The force of wind against the sail will test the knots. Even hot shots work on this.

When you get to the tack, use one of the longer, stronger lines and go twice around the boom, twice through the grommet. Again, use two sail ties if not the longer ones.

When you have the foot of the sail tied to the boom, rig the mast.

Another longer nonstretchy line ties the tack to the mast. Be sure to go twice around the mast and through the tack grommet or use two sail ties. This spot is a place where you need to make sure the sail is tied on tightly.

You have left a little space between the foot and the boom, and you want to leave less space between luff and mast. Just barely enough to see daylight, about 1 mm of space.

Continue using your shorter ties to secure the luff to the mast, going up to the head of the sail.

Here you need to tie on the halyard and the halyard preventer. The halyard keeps the sail against the mast while the preventer keeps the sail from being pulled over the top of the mast.

Tie the halyard by threading your sail tie through the grommet at the head of the sail and then around the mast twice, passing through the eyestrap on the front of the mast. You want the sail to allow just a glimpse of daylight here.

Tie the halyard preventer so the measurement band on the sail falls within the limits shown by the bands on the mast. If you've tied it too loosely, the sail will rise above the bands when you put on the sprit. If it's too tight, the sail won't go up high enough.

On your mast, run a line through the block secured to the front. Feed the line down through the cleat on the front of the mast. Some people continue the line up through a second block, and back, to make adjusting the line easier. Using a small bowline on the end of the line that comes forward out of the block, catch the sprit end. Use a handle to make it easier to adjust this line.

We recommend the sprit be tied to the starboard side. This will help you know which tack you are on.

This all takes patience and practice, but it is absolutely worth it. Be a careful rigger, and your boat will sail better, and faster!

Now you can put your rig in the boat. Just pick up the mast and carefully guide it through the mast thwart into the mast step. Some people prefer to rig the sprit after the mast has been **stepped** (put in the mast thwart).

Tie the mast in tight with the mast tie-in line and make sure the mast sits firmly in the mast step, and that it does not lift or shake. The step should be adjusted so that the boom is at right angles to the boat. Adjust by turning the thumbscrew to move the mast. You can measure this movement. Push the mast as far aft as you can. Using a tape measure, start at the top of the mast and measure back to the curve in the transom. This should be 112 inches. Lighter sailors (less than 85 pounds) benefit from having the mast **raked** (tipped) slightly aft, to measure 111.5 inches. Heavier sailors (over 99 pounds) can carry a forward rake, measuring 112.5 inches.

Rig the mainsheet parts to the bridle using the snap-on block, or use another kind of attachment like a bowline or a shackle. Some people feel that a snap-on block can be a problem because it can hook your life jacket when the boom changes sides. Don't forget to run the vang line through the cleat!

Make sure all your knots are secure.

Make sure you have tied on the mast tie line so that your mast will stay in the boat if you capsize.

Make sure your main sheet is running free (not tied down tightly).

The amount of rake is the angle from the top of the mast toward the transom. If the top of the mast tilts backward, this is aft rake. If it tilts forward, it is called forward rake.

Changes in Course

Before you decide which point of sail you are going to try, you need to be familiar with some more nautical terms.

To **head up** or to **point higher** is to turn the boat more in the direction the wind is coming from.

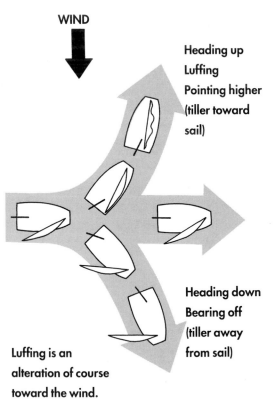

WIND

Heading up
Luffing
Pointing higher
(tiller toward sail)

Heading down
Bearing off
(tiller away from sail)

Luffing is an alteration of course toward the wind.

To **head down** or to **bear off** is to turn the boat away from where the wind is coming from.

A **lift** is a windshift that lets you point higher.

A **header** is a windshift that makes you bear off.

To stop the boat, ease your sail all the way out with the wind coming across the side of the boat. This is called the **safety position.**

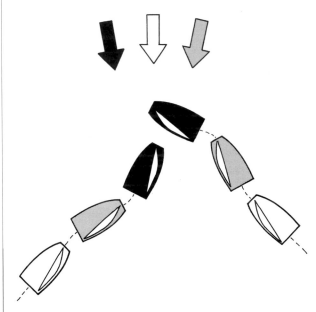

When the wind shifts direction, you sail at different angles. A *lift* allows you to head up. A *header* makes you bear off away from your course. It is important to note that a *lift* on one tack is a *header* on the other tack.

Basic Tips

Here are some basic sailing tips that you should know before you launch your boat.

Where Do You Sit When Sailing?

Always sit facing the sail. You need to know whether the sail is full or luffing, and you can see it better this way.

Sit just behind the bulkhead. For your first sail, you won't be going out in a lot of wind, so you should be comfortable sitting inside the boat.

How Do You Hold the Tiller?

In the hand closest to the stern. Hold it firmly but gently with your fingers on the end of the hiking stick. No need to grab on to it too hard. You want to use smooth, even movements when you move the tiller. Try not to saw back and forth. To help yourself steer straight, rest your hand on your knee. Remember to hold the tiller like a microphone.

How Do You Hold the Mainsheet?

In the hand closest to the bow. Keep your little finger closest to the mainsheet block. Rest your mainsheet hand on the other knee to help relax. Do not wrap it around your hand or put it in your mouth.

How Do You Turn the Boat?

With the tiller. If you push the tiller toward the sail, the boat will turn in the opposite direction, which will be toward the wind.

When you steer, always face the tiller and keep your arms parallel to your legs. If you push the tiller toward the sail, the boat turns into the wind.

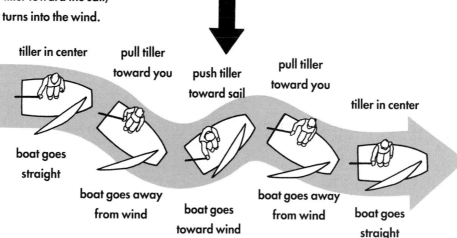

tiller in center — boat goes straight

pull tiller toward you — boat goes away from wind

push tiller toward sail — boat goes toward wind

pull tiller toward you — boat goes away from wind

tiller in center — boat goes straight

If you pull the tiller away from the sail, the boat will turn toward the sail, again in the opposite direction and away from the wind.

If you keep the tiller in the middle of the boat, you will sail straight ahead.

The rudder is very big in proportion to the size of an Optimist hull, so even the smallest steering changes greatly affect the direction of the boat. Steer as little as is necessary. There are exceptions to this rule: when you are trying to avoid a sudden jibe, for instance, you will want to push the tiller hard toward the sail.

The engine: a luffing sail means your engine is in neutral. To get the boat moving, put it in gear by trimming in the mainsheet and steering away from the wind until the sail fills.

Your boat will accelerate and sail forward when you fill your sail with wind.

Launching

You can launch an Optimist from a dock, from a ramp, or from the beach.

From the dock, ask a few friends to help lift, then lower, the boat into the water. Don't rush; you don't want to swamp the boat at the dock! If you do swamp it, bail, bail, bail.

Use three or more people to carry your boat.

Many hands make light work. It is easier with three launching the Optimist.

From a ramp, use a dolly and just roll it in.

From the beach, get two friends to help you carry the boat (one of you at the bow, the other two at each corner of the transom).

Do not drag your boat across the sand or ground. Carry the boat. When you put the boat in the water, stand on the side of the boat away from the land. Never stay between a boat and breaking waves on the shore. A big wave could push the boat—and you—onto the shore.

Turn the boat sideways to the wind and climb aboard. Grab on to a hiking strap and haul yourself in. Think about balance. Try not to capsize and you won't.

If you have to step into your boat from a dock, step to the center of the boat, behind the bulkhead. Keep your daggerboard down for stability. These are stable boats, but you do want to remember that your weight makes a difference!

If someone is in the water holding your boat while you get ready to sail, now is the time to put the rudder on. As soon as you are in the boat, make sure your rudder is locked down.

Put your daggerboard down at least halfway.

Turn your boat so that the wind is coming across the side of the boat. Use your mainsheet to pull in your sail. Keep your tiller in the middle of the boat, and off you go!

WINDWARD SHORE TIPS

If launching from a windward shore (the wind is blowing off the land onto the water), put your daggerboard halfway down, turn your boat around, make sure your mainsheet is free. When it fills with wind, trim the mainsheet, and off you go.

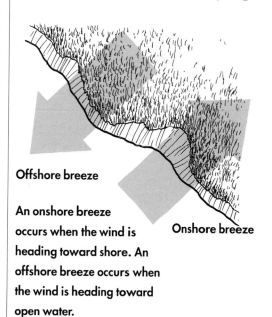

Offshore breeze

An onshore breeze occurs when the wind is heading toward shore. An offshore breeze occurs when the wind is heading toward open water.

Onshore breeze

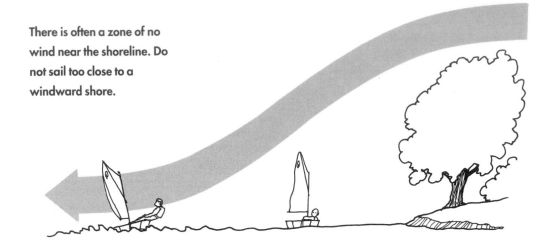

There is often a zone of no wind near the shoreline. Do not sail too close to a windward shore.

Remember that the land protects you from some of the wind, so be prepared for a stronger breeze when you get out of the land's **windshadow.**

LEEWARD SHORE TIPS

For a first sail, this is a better breeze, because the wind will blow you back on shore. The wind on a leeward shore is blowing from the water to the land. But it makes it a little harder to get started.

Keep your mainsheet free while you are getting in your boat. Turn your bow around until it is pointing a little away from the direction of the wind. Climb in, and put your daggerboard all the way down. Pull in your mainsheet until your sail fills, tiller in the center of the boat, and . . . you're sailing!

If you need to stop, steer your boat into the safety position with the wind from the side and your sail all the way out.

If you want to go faster, pull your sail in and you will speed up.

FINAL PREPARATION

Take a tip from airline pilots and Olympic sailors: after you have launched your boat, cleared your mooring, or sailed off the dock, take a minute to check everything out before you proceed. A sailor who knows that everything is in its place and working properly sails better because he doesn't have to wonder about any of that as he's sailing along.

On the Water

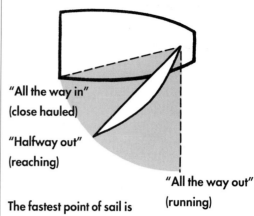

"All the way in"
(close hauled)

"Halfway out"
(reaching)

"All the way out"
(running)

The fastest point of sail is reaching. The sail will be eased out halfway.

SAILING ON A REACH

The easiest point of sailing is a reach. You are facing the sail, the wind is coming over the side of the boat (turn your face into the wind to make sure you know where it's coming from).

You have adjusted the mainsheet so that the sail is full of wind (no wrinkles, no luffing), and you are steering with the tiller.

If your sail starts luffing, pull the tiller a little away from the sail until the luffing stops. Just a little at a time. Easy does it. If you feel the boat **heeling** (tipping) too much in the direction of the sail, let your sail out a little until you are sailing flat again.

On a reach, your sail will be about halfway out.

"Halfway out to where?" you ask.

On a sailboat, having a sail "all the way out" means at right angles to the boat. On an Optimist, having your sail "all the way in" means having it so that the boom is just over the leeward corner of the transom, or the **quarter.** On a reach, the boom should be halfway between these two places.

When steering, a good rule of thumb to use is to point the **tiller toward trouble.** If you are heading for another boat and you might have a collision, pushing the tiller at the other boat will make you steer away from the problem.

Reaching in an Optimist can be a very fast point of sail. Enjoy it!

TACKING

You know that a boat cannot sail directly to a spot that is exactly where the wind is coming from, because a sailboat cannot sail directly into the wind. (This is the no-go zone.) But by **tacking,** a sailboat can get to this spot that is straight into the wind.

Tacking means zigzagging back and forth, each time getting a little closer to where the wind is coming from.

This boat is on starboard tack. The wind is coming over the starboard (right) side and the boom is on the port (left) side. The side the wind is coming over is also called the windward side. The side the boom is on is called the leeward side.

To tack, you push the tiller toward the sail until the bow passes through the wind and the sail shifts to the other side of the boat.

This can be confusing. **Tack** is both a verb and a noun. You turn the boat (tack) to put the sail and the wind on the other side of the bow, which is called the other tack.

• If the sail is on the right side, the boat is on the **port tack,** because the wind is coming over the port (left) side of the boat.

• If the sail is on the left side, the boat is on the **starboard tack** because the wind is coming over the starboard (right) side.

As the sail comes over to the other side, you change sides, too, so you can still sit facing the sail.

When you change sides, you also change hands holding the tiller and the mainsheet. We like to face forward during a tack. Always hold on to the mainsheet with one hand or the other.

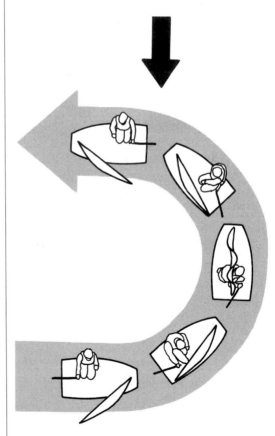

When you sail from one reach to the other, you will be heading back in the direction from which you came.

Here is a step-by-step approach:

1. Slowly push the tiller toward the sail.

2. Put one foot across to the other side while facing forward.

3. As the boat turns and the sail and boom move to the middle of the boat, duck your head.

4. Move quickly to the other side of the boat and sit down.

5. Take your mainsheet hand behind your back and hold the tiller with that hand at the same time.

6. Quickly take the old tiller hand and grab the mainsheet.

7. Steer the boat on the desired new course.

Once the bow has come through the

One way to find the wind direction is to face the wind and turn your head back and forth, feeling the wind pressure on your ears. When the pressure is the same on each side, you are facing straight into the wind.

wind and the sail has filled on the new side, straighten the tiller and sail on the other reach. It helps to have an object on land or an object on the water to head for after you have made a maneuver.

Again, feel where the wind is (when you are facing directly into the wind, you will feel the breeze blowing evenly past your ears). If you try to straighten the tiller out before your bow and sail get all the way through the wind, your bow will stay stubbornly pointed right into the wind. Your sail will luff and you won't be able to steer in the "no-go zone."

RUNNING

When the wind is directly behind you, you are running, or on a run. Your boat is being pushed by the wind from behind. This can be a lot of fun, because you are moving with the waves.

To start a run, gently pull the tiller away from the sail and ease your sail out until it is at right angles to (pointing straight across) the hull.

You want the wind to stay behind you; you do not want to turn your stern through the wind, so pay attention here.

If you feel as if the sail might be about to change sides (it will do this very quickly once it starts) push the tiller toward the sail, then straighten the tiller back to the center. You can do this in a very fast little jerk of a motion. This will keep your stern from turning through the wind and causing a **jibe**.

One of the greatest thrills in sailing is surfing a wave and dramatically increasing your speed.

Sailing by the lee occurs when the wind is coming from the leeward side of the boat. This could be a dangerous situation because the boat can suddenly jibe. Usually sailing by the lee is slow in an Optimist, and should be done by experienced sailors.

A boat sails better and faster on a run

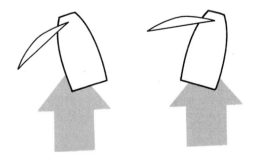

When the wind is hitting your boat from the leeward side, you are sailing by the lee.

without the interference of the daggerboard, and as you practice, you will pull it up. But until you are comfortable on a run, you should keep it halfway down.

JIBING

There is another way to change direction in a sailboat. Instead of turning your bow through the wind, you turn your stern through the wind.

Jibing is faster and a little trickier than tacking. You do not want to jibe unless you are ready. Control your boat. *You* decide when to jibe.

The wind catches the sail by the leech when you jibe, and because the luff is attached to the stationary mast, the wind whips the sail across the boat.

But jibing really is easy to do, once you know how.

Change directions when you are going *downwind* by jibing. Your sail is well out, and your daggerboard is at least halfway down if you are on your first sail. Later, it might be all the way up.

To get ready to jibe, grab the mainsheet parts about a foot and a half down from the boom.

Pull the boom over your head (duck!) as you pull the tiller away from the sail. This turns your stern through the wind. As the sail fills on the other side, quickly and smoothly move to the other side of the boat. Straighten out the tiller until you are on the desired new course.

When jibing, trim the mainsheet just as the boom passes over your head.

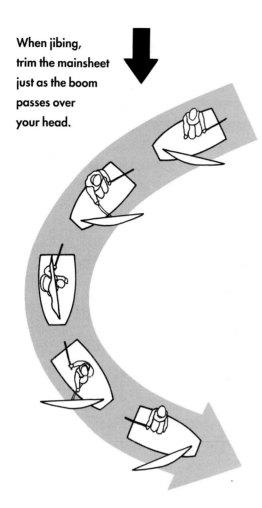

Exchange hands on the tiller and mainsheet. The key is to control the mainsheet and the tiller during your maneuver. By facing forward you will see where you are heading.

If you want to point closer to the wind and sail on a reach, all you have to do is pull in the mainsheet, push the tiller toward the sail, then straighten out the tiller after the sail passes through the wind. You are now on a reach.

UPWIND

If you want to sail to a place that is directly upwind, you know you can't go straight for it. You have to get there by making a series of tacks in that direction.

You can do this on a reach, or a close reach, but it will take you a long time. It is shorter to **beat** or sail **close hauled.**

This means sailing as close to where the wind is coming from as you can.

If you are reaching, and you want to sail close hauled, start by pulling in your mainsheet until the end of your boom is just over the quarter (this is the back corner on the same side as your sail).

When you want to sail in the direction the wind is coming from, you must tack back and forth on a close-hauled course. Reaching may be the faster point of sail, but it will take much longer to sail to windward.

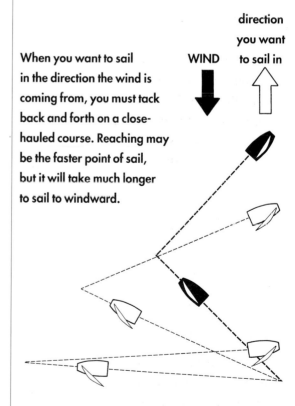

direction you want to sail in

WIND

Sit in a position on your boat that keeps the hull level with the water.

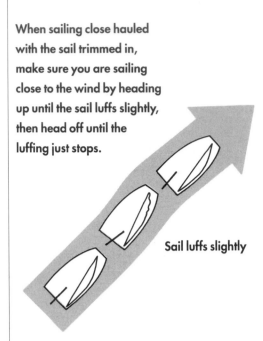

When sailing close hauled with the sail trimmed in, make sure you are sailing close to the wind by heading up until the sail luffs slightly, then head off until the luffing just stops.

Sail luffs slightly

Then push the tiller toward the sail smoothly just until you see your sail start to luff. The shaking will start along the luff of the sail, which is why it's called a luff. As soon as the sail starts to shake, pull the tiller away from the sail just a little until the luffing stops, then bring the tiller back to the middle of the boat.

On a beat, you will sit forward, unless your bow is plowing into the waves. But remember that you want to keep the boat as flat as you can with all four corners as far out of the water as possible.

This means you must pay attention not only to which side you are sitting on, but to whether you are so far forward that you are making the bow plow into the water, or whether you are so far aft that you are dragging the stern. Try to get a feel for what seems like a good balance. A fine start is to tuck in just behind the bulkhead. Keep your knees together and facing ahead.

In a light breeze, you can sit or squat inside the boat. In a little more wind, you will want to sit on the gunwale.

If the wind picks up even more, you will want to lean out of the boat to keep it flat. This is called **hiking,** and you will need to steer with your tiller extension or **hiking stick.**

Hold your hiking stick with a light grasp. Some sailors prefer to use a few fingers. Remember you are holding the microphone. If you find you are squeezing the hiking stick or tiller too hard, it is an indication that you are very tense. Relax your hold and you will sail better.

Keep your knees facing forward, if you are sitting in the boat, and keep your weight close to the bulkhead. We recommend keeping your arms and legs parallel.

If you are out on the rail, hook your feet under the hiking straps, but still stay close to the bulkhead.

Because the wind is constantly changing direction and speed, even in tiny amounts, you need to keep trying to see if you are sailing as close hauled as possible.

You do this by gently pushing the tiller toward the sail until the sail luffs. To stop

As your skills improve, sailing in strong winds will become fun.

it from luffing, pull the tiller away from the sail a little. This way, you keep testing to see whether you are as **high** as you can be.

If you are too high on the wind, your sail will luff. And if you are sailing along almost luffing, you are slower than you need to be. This is called **pinching.** Head down a little (pull the tiller away from the sail) and catch more wind in your sail. You will feel your boat speed up.

Sail along on a beat for a while, then change tacks . . . by tacking!

In a good breeze, beating back and forth is how you will get back to a windward shore. It's fun and exciting to be able to change tacks close hauled!

LANDING

When you are coming in from a sail, decide whether you are landing on a windward or leeward shore.

If the wind is blowing onto the land, it's a leeward shore. To land on a leeward shore:

Sail in toward land on a run. Remember, the faster you turn your boat, the faster it will stop. A slow turn allows you to coast for a longer distance and keep control. Remember that to stop your Optimist, you just let out your sail. If you need to stop fast, ease the mainsheet quickly.

Always hold on to the mainsheet, so you don't lose control, in case you need to start sailing again quickly.

As you get close to shore, turn your bow into the wind by pushing the tiller toward the sail.

When the boom is over the center of the boat, unclip the mainsheet and put it in the bottom of the boat.

As you turn back toward the land, take your daggerboard out of the daggerboard trunk and put it on the bottom of the boat.

Reach over the transom and take off the rudder.

By now, you should have blown close enough to shore to jump out. Hold your boat and walk it up to the shore.

If the wind is blowing off the land, then you are landing on a windward shore.

To land on a windward shore, sail to windward toward shore (widow help) until the water isn't over your head.

Free the mainsheet (just let it go) and take out the daggerboard.

Reach around and take out the rudder.

Unclip the mainsheet parts. Now you should be close enough to shore to climb overboard and pull your boat to the beach or ramp.

To land at a dock, always try to pick a spot where you will approach the dock pointing directly into the wind. Sometimes it helps to sail by the dock to survey the best place to land. Make a pass or two to see where that might be.

Approach a dock head into the wind and arrive at an angle so you can reach out and hold on to the dock.

Once you have selected your spot on the dock, sail to a point about two to three boatlengths to leeward and then round into the wind. Once into the wind, ease the mainsheet. The best sailors are always smooth when landing. Gary learned years ago in the navy that you will make good landings if you never yell and you always approach slowly.

If you don't think you are going to reach the dock, trim your sail and circle around for a second attempt. This is a good maneuver to practice. You will gain confidence when you practice docking maneuvers.

Once you reach the dock, use your bowline to tie up. Make sure your bowline is attached to the boat. Only use the space you need. Avoid rubbing or banging up against other boats.

Once you have landed successfully and your boat is secured to the dock, help the next sailor tie up.

ACCELERATION, SLOWING DOWN, AND STOPPING

Optimists are very responsive boats. This means that they do what you ask very quickly. You will soon learn that you do not have to push or pull the tiller very hard to have the boat head up or bear away from the wind. The faster you are sailing, the easier it is to turn. It is difficult to maneuver a boat that is moving slowly.

To accelerate and get your boat moving forward, trim in your sail and at the same time pull the tiller toward the windward side of the boat (away from the sail). Sit in the middle of the boat. Move on to the side if the wind is blowing and the boat starts to heel to leeward. It takes an Optimist about five boatlengths to accelerate up to full speed. Heavier boats with keels take longer.

If you have a short distance to sail before you must maneuver, always try to bear off away from the wind to gain speed before making your maneuver.

When you trim your mainsheet, the boat will naturally round up into the wind. So as you trim, keep your hand on the tiller and pull it to windward (away from the sail) at the same time.

Once you are sailing, always watch where you are heading very carefully. If you have to change course quickly to avoid another boat or an object in the water, it helps if you are sailing at full speed because sailboats maneuver easier when they are moving fast.

As we mentioned earlier, you can avoid collisions by moving the "tiller toward trouble."

Slowing an Optimist into the safety position is easy: just let go of the mainsheet and let the sail luff. Soon the boat will drift to a stop. Again, keep the boat on a beam reach so the sail is away from your head and so the boat does not move backwards.

Stopping your boat quickly is

Five different ways to slow down

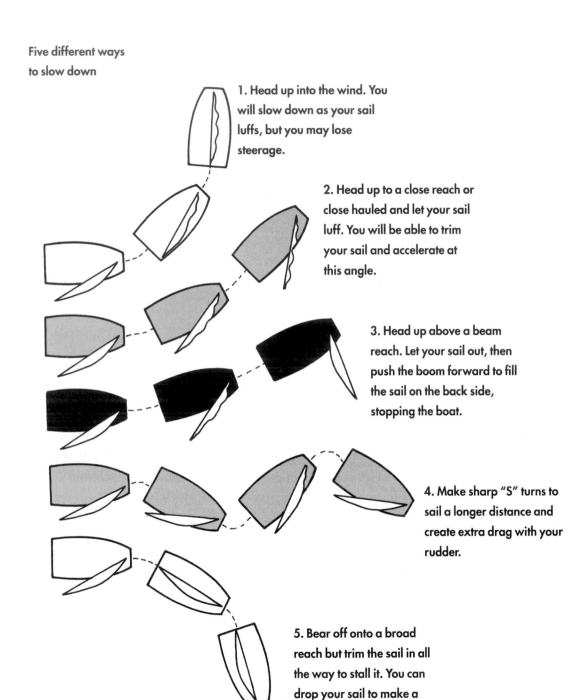

1. Head up into the wind. You will slow down as your sail luffs, but you may lose steerage.

2. Head up to a close reach or close hauled and let your sail luff. You will be able to trim your sail and accelerate at this angle.

3. Head up above a beam reach. Let your sail out, then push the boom forward to fill the sail on the back side, stopping the boat.

4. Make sharp "S" turns to sail a longer distance and create extra drag with your rudder.

5. Bear off onto a broad reach but trim the sail in all the way to stall it. You can drop your sail to make a downwind landing.

Back your sail to slow the boat down.

important. You can stop by heading straight into the wind until your sails luff, then push the boom out to windward to backwind the sail, or let it fill backwards. If you lose all forward momentum, the boat will be difficult to steer. You are now in "irons" or in the "no-go zone."

SAILING OUT OF THE NO-GO ZONE

Many sailors end up in the no-go zone or "in irons." It happens to everyone at one time or another. This means the boat is stopped, heading directly into the wind and having lost all headway. You can end up in the no-go zone if the wind shifts direction. The boat will not sail off on either tack.

Not to worry. Being caught in irons is an everyday occurrence. Just be patient. Relax. Take your time getting out of irons: no one is going to attack your sailboat with a cannon.

There are two ways to get out of irons. The first is to put your tiller hard over to one side. You will drift backwards a bit, and your sail will move over to whichever side of the boat your tiller is pointing as your bow moves to that same side of the wind. Sheet in gently, center your tiller, and you're moving ahead again.

For instance, if you put your tiller hard to port, your sail will start to move from luffing (flapping) in the middle of the boat toward the port side. As soon as your bow is definitely on the port side of where the wind is coming from, pull in your mainsheet until it stops luffing, pull the tiller toward the center of the boat, away from the side the sail is on, and you will be off and sailing forward on the starboard tack.

The other way to get out of irons is to backwind your sail: hold the boom out over to one side of the boat and hold your tiller to the other side. You will go backwards! When your boat is moving astern you steer in the opposite direction from when the boat was moving ahead. As your bow starts to move out of the no-go zone, release the sail (it will cross the boat, so duck!). When the boat is on the desired course, trim in your mainsheet and straighten your tiller. And off you go.

Anytime you need to maneuver, accelerate, slow down, stop, or get out of irons, the key is to use the rudder in combination with your weight and the sail to help control and steer your Optimist.

When using your weight, moving aft will force the boat into the wind. Moving forward will force the boat away from the wind. Trimming your sail forces you toward the wind, while easing your sail helps you bear away from the wind.

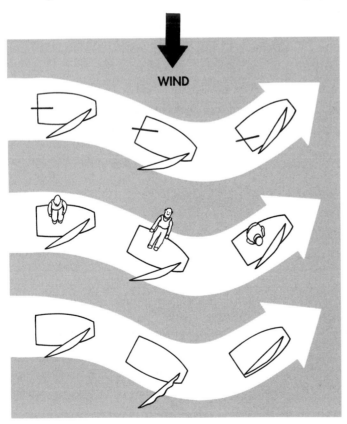

WIND

Starting position　　**To bear off**　　**To head up**

There are three ways to turn your boat. Reading the columns from top to bottom, use any one or all three in combination.

To bear off, 1) pull the tiller away from the sail, 2) heel the boat to windward, or 3) ease the sail.

To head up, 1) push the tiller toward the sail, 2) heel to leeward or 3) trim the sail.

Remember not to use too much tiller, which slows you down.

Weather Awareness

READING THE WIND

You need wind to sail. The pressure of the wind against the sail is the "engine" that powers your Optimist.

Since you can't see the wind, how can you tell where it's coming from?

It's easy. Look at the way flags are blowing. Check out the way boats are lying at their moorings. They'll face into the wind. Look for smoke from smokestacks, see if the trees are blowing in one direction. Of course, if they are really bending in the breeze, chances are it's blowing too hard for you to go out!

The best way to know about the wind is to try to learn to feel it on your face. If you pay attention to this, and think about how a light breeze feels, a stronger breeze, too much breeze, soon you will be able to tune and sail your boat accordingly.

To tell where the wind is coming from, turn around slowly until you can tell that the wind is blowing directly on your face. Some sailors claim that they can feel a lift or a header coming because they feel the

How may different ways can you learn the direction of the wind from this drawing? (Answer: Masthead fly, luffing sail, feel of wind on face, flag, smoke from stacks, angles of other boats sailing, ripples on the water)

wind more in their ears instead of on their cheeks.

How to Read the Wind

1. Look at one section of the horizon at a time.

2. Use sunglasses to help contrast the color of the water.

3. Let your eyes blink naturally. Don't squint.

4. Contrast the differences in the color of the water to a constant color like your sails or your boat.

5. Stand up in your boat so you can see farther.

6. Study the patterns.

7. Use all sources available (other boats, flags, ripples on the water, smokestacks, etc.).

When you are on the water, you need to be able to know what the wind is doing, and you need to be able to have a good guess about what it is going to do.

There are various wind indicators on your boat (masthead fly, telltales on your sail), and they work to tell you different things as you sail along. But the wind is always changing patterns, and you want to be able to identify what they are.

Look for ripples on the water. Sometimes the wind does not affect the waves or the ripples instantly, but you can see where there is no wind (a slick, flat patch), and you can see where a little breeze might be building (an increase in the breeze puts more ripples on the water, which makes the water look darker, so you can see a puff coming).

Check the other boats. See where they are heading, how they have their sails adjusted.

There are lots of old sayings about the weather, and sometimes they prove true. It can't hurt to think about them. "Red skies at morning, sailors take warning! Red skies at night, sailors delight." Or "Rain before wind, take her in. Wind before rain, set sail again." Cornelius Shields, a very famous and experienced sailor, wrote about these sailors' observations: Wind from the northeast generally brings rain, at least on the East Coast. Dew in the morning means an early, strong, southerly wind. And this one seems a little weird, but here it is: "Cobwebs in the rigging means a northwester in the near future."

Listen to the marine weather forecast on the radio, or watch the Weather Channel on television, and find out whether you'll have a good day for a sail. Never go out if you can see lightning, and make sure there will be a safety boat paying attention to you.

Remember that the shoreline can affect the wind. Just as water flows around obstacles, the wind blows around them, too. Sailing near a shoreline where the trees are tall will affect the wind.

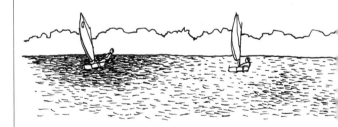

Look at the small ripples on the water. More wind causes more ripples and looks darker. Less wind means fewer ripples. Look at the boats ahead. Boats in more wind heel more, or the skippers are hiking harder.

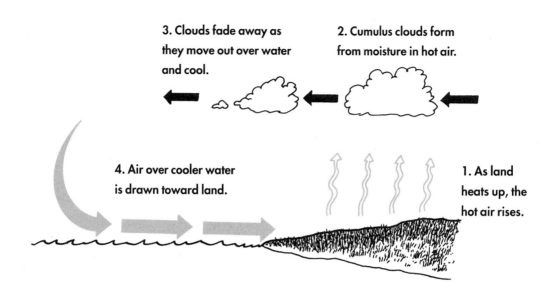

3. Clouds fade away as they move out over water and cool.

2. Cumulus clouds form from moisture in hot air.

4. Air over cooler water is drawn toward land.

1. As land heats up, the hot air rises.

Sailing close to other boats also affects the wind that your boat will (or won't!) feel.

If the obstacle is tall enough, you can be **blanketed.** That means all the wind is blocked by the obstacle, and you will lose your "engine," the wind.

The wind has patterns. In some places, there will be a sea breeze that blows toward the shore each afternoon. This is because as the day has gone on, the land has warmed up and has caused the air to rise above it. This draws in the air over cooler water. And that's thermal wind: air that is pulled or pushed from one place to another because of differences in temperature.

The wind also moves according to the earth's rotations, so you know that in the Northern Hemisphere the wind tends to travel counterclockwise and inward toward a low-pressure center, and low-pressure centers tend to move toward the east.

Therefore, the wind will veer (shift to the right) when the low passes to the north, and then shift back (to the left) when the low passes to the south. This usually happens when a cold front is predicted.

The low that comes before the cold front will cause an abrupt windshift from the southwest to the northeast, and it will get chilly. This is when you can expect thunderstorms and really wild windshifts.

As a storm approaches, the wind will usually die down. Don't be fooled by this! This is just the lull before the storm or squall hits. Powerful gusts will follow from the direction of the storm, because of the heavy rain within the storm. As the heavy rain arrives, the wind will usually

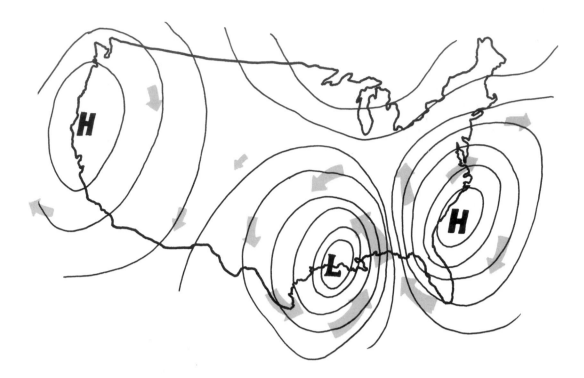

die down. Just be patient and you can sail as soon as the storm passes.

Weather Sources

1. Newspaper
2. Weather radio—National Oceanographic Atmospheric Administration (NOAA)
3. Advice of local sailors
4. Cable television
5. The Internet
6. Weather maps
7. Commercial radio
8. Network television
9. Your own observation

Wind moves counterclockwise and inward around a low-pressure system and clockwise and outward around a high-pressure system. Isobars are drawn on a weather chart connecting areas of equal pressure. The closer isobars are together, the greater the pressure difference and the stronger the wind.

The circulation of winds around a depression is counterclockwise in the Northern Hemisphere and clockwise in the Southern Hemisphere.

Waves, Current, and Tides

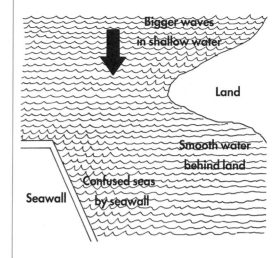

WAVES

Waves slow your boat, especially short, steep ones. Smoother water is found in the lee of land, breakwaters, and deeper waters. The interval between waves gets shorter as the water gets shallower.

Avoid areas where the waves break against the shore, a brackwater, or docks where the resulting confused seas will slow you down. The wind tends to be confused here, too.

When you are tuning up before the start, notice if the angle of the waves is the same or different on both tacks. If it is different, you will have to trim your sail differently on each tack.

If you find that on one tack you are heading more directly into the waves, then you must trim for power.

Reaching in waves is a blast! You want to follow waves down when you can catch a surf (like the second boat), then head up onto a faster course when you lose your wave while looking for the next wave to catch. You can pump your sail once per wave to help start the surf.

If you find that on the other tack you are sailing across the waves, you might choose to head higher and trim for direction rather than speed.

Since waves really affect an Optimist, spend at least fifteen minutes before a race checking them out. Waves generally have a pattern. Think about how you will time your wave-riding techniques, and get into the rhythm of it.

Keeping your boat balanced and your sails working through the waves is most important. Pump (once!) to catch a ride on a big wave, try to power through the troughs where there is less wind, and aim for staying on top or on the front face of the waves.

CURRENT

Current is the movement of water caused by the action of the tides, by wind, by rainfall, by surges in the level of water, or even by other boats.

If the current is the same all over a race course, for example, you only have to consider how it will affect your boat at the start (push you over early; hold you below the line), or during mark roundings (carry you into the mark; lift you above the layline; keep you under the layline).

But if the current varies from place to place on the course, you need to plan your race accordingly. Downwind, as a rule, sail against the current early in the leg, so that you will have more speed

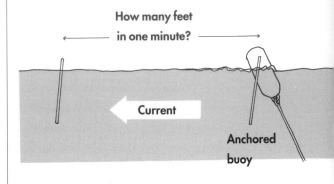

How many feet in one minute?

Current

Anchored buoy

To measure current, place a floating object next to an anchored buoy. Start your watch and see how far the current pushes the object in one minute. That's also how far it will push your boat each minute. See if you can measure the current on different parts of the course.

sailing with the current as you approach the next mark.

You can determine what the current is doing by looking at any object in the water that is anchored to the bottom. A small wake will trail a buoy or a float or a mark. You can judge both the direction (called the **set**) and the speed (called the **drift**) of currents by observing these little wakes.

You can also see differences in current by looking at the water surface. When the current is against the wind, there will be more surface friction and choppier waves. The opposite is true when current runs with the wind. The water will be much smoother.

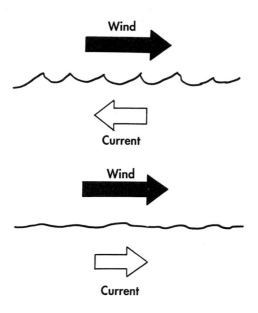

When the current opposes the wind, the waves are much choppier than when the current is flowing with the wind.

Current Strength Table

Feet/Minute	Knots of Current
10	0.1
20	0.2
30	0.3
40	0.4
50	0.5
100	1.0

This table demonstrates how current alone can affect your boat. For example: in one minute, if the current is 1 knot, your boat can drift 100 feet.

Tide and current charts help plan your race. Check them out. The current is usually stronger in deeper channels, and here the tide will have a strengthening effect as well.

Wind also has an effect on the current. If the wind is with the current, for example, it can delay the time at which the tide changes.

TIDES

Tide does not refer to the movement of the water. It is a measurement of depth. But of course the current (movement) caused by the incoming or outgoing or changing tide affects your boat.

Fine-Tuning Your Skills

PART IV

Going Faster

Rigging the Racing Rig

A racing Optimist has more go-fast gear than a club rig, allowing you to gain more speed from your boat and also control it better.

MAST STEP ADJUSTMENTS

The tolerances of your mast step adjustments are strictly determined by class rules. Your mast step should fit snugly to the floor of your boat, and should not lift or shake back and forth.

The goal here is to try to keep the boom parallel to the water. You do not want it to be able to move significantly sideways, either.

A cup-fitted mast step is best for holding your mast steady, especially in rough water or strong wind. The cup fittings put less pressure on the small plastic mast-end caps and on weaker masts.

Mast step cups should slide easily when the thumbscrew is turned, so keep them lubricated! And rinse salt off them after every sail.

GENERAL ADJUSTMENTS

It is not necessary to adjust the rake of your mast for every different breeze. It is better to rig your mast at a 90-degree angle. (Use a credit card or any square card like a library card on the mast thwart: hold it sideways up against the mast. You will easily see where the mast makes a square angle to the boat this way).

For a light sailor (under seventy-five pounds), a one-degree rake aft could be an advantage.

For a seventy-five- to ninety-pound sailor, a right angle should be tried first.

And for a sailor over ninety pounds, a one-degree rake forward could make a difference.

These adjustments can only be made before a race, not during. So pay attention to the weather conditions, and rake accordingly.

Sail with your boom parallel to your

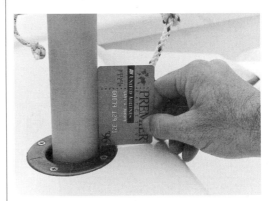

Use a credit card to check that the mast is at a 90-degree angle.

boat. When you feel you have the sail trimmed correctly, ask a sailor on another boat to check the boom's position for you.

HOTSHOT TIPS

Optimist masts will bend in a good breeze, so you can rake your mast slightly forward to help keep your boom parallel to the water, when your mainsheet is trimmed tightly.

SPRIT ADJUSTMENTS

Adjusting your sprit is an important sail-shaping control.

Once your rig is in your boat, start tuning it by tightening your sprit.

You should have an adjuster with a 2-to-1 line (line runs through a block and back), with a comfortable handle attached (a trapeze-type handle), in an easy-to-grab position.

For smaller sailors, attach the cleat higher on the mast. For bigger sailors, the cleat can be lower.

You want your sprit just tight enough to make a gentle wrinkle from sail peak to tack when luffing. This should disappear as soon as you are sailing. If it remains under sail, your sprit is too tight. Loosen (lower) your sprit.

Control the position of your sail (between the measurement bands) by adjusting your sail ties and/or your sprit.

To flatten the leech of your sail for stronger winds, raise your sprit.

To give your leech more bag (when the

If your sprit is not adjusted correctly you will get a crease in the middle of your sail.

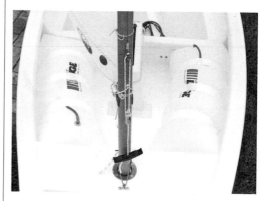

A trapeze-type handle permits easy adjustments to the sprit.

breeze drops), lower your sprit. Don't be dramatic about these adjustments. Ease them on and off.

Sail Shape

You *never* want to develop a curl in the leech of your sail. This happens when the leech is tighter than the middle of the sail. The boat will sail slowly because, when too tight, the trailing edge of the sail acts as a brake.

WHAT IS A GOOD SAIL SHAPE?

You want the wind to have a smooth entry onto your sail at the mast and luff, and a smooth exit off the leech. The faster the wind flows across the sail, and the smoother it leaves the leech, the faster you will go.

The bulging part of your sail, called draft, should be in the center.

If your luff is too tight, or the sprit is too tight, you will have a bulge close to your mast. This will keep you from pointing as close to the wind as you might.

If your sprit is too loose or the luff is too loose, you will develop a curl that will slow you right down!

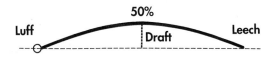

Cross Section of Sail

Learn to adjust your sail for the wind conditions.

If it is a moderate breeze, you can maintain a lower sprit and a looser outhaul.

In strong breezes, raise the sprit and tighten the outhaul.

TELLTALES

The masthead fly is the best wind indicator on the Optimist dinghy. Some Optimist sailors have had success using telltales on their sails. But telltales can cause considerable confusion.

If using a telltale on the luff, if the leeward telltale luffs you are overtrimmed, and if the inside or windward telltale luffs you are undertrimmed.

Some sailors use too many telltales and have difficulty following the action of the wind in the sail. The most important places are at the front of the sail and at the end of each batten.

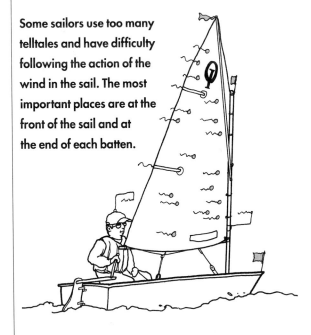

OTHER SAIL SHAPE CONTROLLERS

Vang

When your vang is tight, you are holding the boom down in a way that will flatten the luff and the leech of your sail. On an Optimist, the vang acts as a downhaul, as well as giving your boom a slight curve. But if your vang is too tight, and if you don't have twists on your boom preventer, you will create a very flat entry for your sail. This will reduce your power.

The vang is critical downwind in a strong breeze. In moderate wind, you won't need anything more than a lightly snugged vang on the wind, and just enough on the run to prevent sail twist. In light air, use just enough vang to keep the boom from raising up.

Outhaul

In a light breeze, ease your outhaul to make a nice full sail shape. As the wind picks up, tighten your outhaul. This will keep your leech nice and flat and help prevent a curl.

Boom Preventer

Don't forget this important adjustment! By putting twists on your boom preventer, you are increasing the draft of your sail along the luff (the boom preventer holds the boom up, remember?). If you weigh over eighty pounds, you will always want twists on the boom preventer, until the wind blows over 20 knots. Now, that would be a fast sail!

A checklist for keeping a fast sail shape:
- Make sure your sprit is not too tight.
- Make sure you don't trim your mainsheet too tight.
- Make sure your vang is eased off.
- Make sure the foot of your sail isn't too baggy.
- Make sure the luff of your sail is properly tied on. Too loose, and you'll ruin the shape of the sail.
- Adjust your outhaul according to the wind speed.
- Shape your sail for the most consistent wind speeds on a particular day. Don't set your sail just for the puffs. You can sail through a puff, but you'll stop dead in the normal breeze if you're depowered for the puffs.
- Check your mast rake. Boom should be parallel to your boat.
- Add twists to your boom preventer

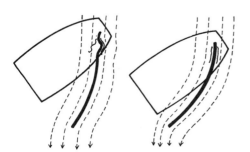

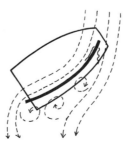

If your sail is overtrimmed, the sail acts as a break and you create a lot of turbulence. If the sail is not trimmed enough it will luff.

to maintain a balanced sail shape according to use of the vang (windspeed and weight-dependent adjustments).

Light Air Sail-shapers (up to 5 knots)

Keep luff and leech on the slack side.

Tie sail on tighter at center of luff, looser toward the head and tack. But keep this an even curve! It takes practice.

Ease luff tension by putting a couple twists in the boom preventer.

Sprit should be off just enough to make a slight crease at the head.

Moderate Breeze Sail-shapers (8 to 10 knots)

Ease outhaul, but not too much. Check for leech curl, which shows up as lumps on the inside edge of the battens.

Keep the boom from going down by putting turns on the boom preventer.

Have sail tied on a straight line at the luff.

Strong Breeze Sail-shapers (15 to 20 knots)

Rake the mast forward to keep the boom parallel to the water. Only rake the mast back if you are severely overpowered.

Rigging Your Mainsheet

A snap shackle will secure your mainsheet parts to your boom bridle. A quick-release is a good idea.

Be sure to choose one that will not catch on your life jacket or clothing when you tack or jibe.

Your boom bridle is an essential piece of your rig. Use wire, Kevlar, or another low-stretch line.

To prevent the bridle from snagging you as you tack or jibe, the ring (to which the mainsheet parts attach) cannot be more than 10 cm from the boom. That's also a class rule.

By having the bridle run along the boom, you make your mainsheet act as a sail-shaper, bending the boom down to open the leech and allow air to spill if you become overpowered.

We recommend using a bridle preventer. This runs from your boom to the mainsheet parts, and takes the load, so it is a good idea for light sailors in a strong breeze. Also, make sure the bridle is held high enough not to get in your way when you tack or jibe.

Tying On Your Sail

This is the most important skill you can learn to maximize your speed. Practice tying your sail on until you can tie it for light, moderate, and heavy airs.

In light air, you want to have the luff looser at the head and tack than along the mast.

Tie the head and tack off about an eighth of an inch. Tie the luff tight in the middle.

In moderate air, tie your sail tightly at

the head and tack, and evenly along the mast, with about a sixteenth of an inch gap between sail and mast.

In heavy air, tie your sail tightly at the tack, but an eighth of an inch off at the head, and evenly along the mast.

Tie on your boom preventer after you have tied on the luff.

After you have rigged your boat once, you will probably keep the luff ties on your sail. When you remove your mast from your boat after a sail, you can just roll your sail, keeping the battens straight, around your boom.

The next time you rig, you will slip the mast down through the luff ties and into the boom jaws, but remember to check to see if your sail ties need retightening or adjusting each time.

Try to adjust your sails so that they are tuned for you and the wind.

For a sailor under 75 pounds, keep your sail flat up high.

For a sailor between 75 and 115 pounds, keep a slight fullness down low.

For sailors over 115 pounds, aim for a fuller sail.

Sailing to Windward

Sailing upwind is exciting. The wind is in your face and the boat is working its way through the waves like a car driving over a series of hills. It's good exercise, too. In a good breeze, you will want to be hiking out on the windward side. Builds good stomach and leg muscles!

Sit facing your sail, with the wind at your back, keeping the mainsheet in your forward hand and the hiking stick in your back hand. Hold the mainsheet with your thumb up. This gives you greater control over the small or big sail adjustments you might need as the wind shifts.

To get the most out of sailing your Optimist to windward, you want to keep the boat flat, causing the blades and rig to work most efficiently. This means you will want to heel the boat so that it is sailing on one of its edges, not the wide flat bottom.

Keep the boat heeled to windward slightly. This will keep more of the sail higher up in the air, to catch more wind.

Pounding in waves can slow you down when you sail to windward, so keep shifting your weight (moving your body) backward and forward to keep your boat moving evenly ahead.

You will never have to pull your mainsheet in beyond the leeward corner of your transom.

Keep your daggerboard all the way down, unless you are a very light sailor. Then it can help in a very strong breeze

As a puff hits, hike out and ease your sail to keep the boat as flat as you can . . . and of course, try not to get any spray in your eyes!

to pull your daggerboard up just a little to depower your sail. This will keep you going faster forward.

Your goal is to sail as close to the wind as possible without luffing. You want to find "the groove," that course where the boat is going as fast as possible, as close to the wind as possible. Because the wind does shift and change, you have to keep testing your course.

Remember that you do not have to yank your tiller back and forth to do this. Keep a steady, light hand on the tiller and make small adjustments to see if the wind will allow you to head up. The Optimist has a big rudder in proportion to its size,

so just a little pressure from the helmsman is enough to turn the boat. *You* control the boat!

If your sails start to luff, bear away a little by pulling the tiller away from the sail. Straighten the tiller out as soon as your sail is full, and keep on testing your course close to the wind.

Because your boat sails best when the wind is flowing evenly over the sail, and when the boat is as flat as possible, you can control sudden puffs of wind with your weight and with sail controls. In puffy wind, ease your sail, hike out more, and head up toward the wind. The combination of all three makes efficient upwind sailing.

If you have a strong **windward helm** (you feel a strong pull on the tiller away from you, toward the sail), try flattening the boat with your weight and heading up

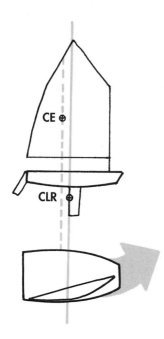

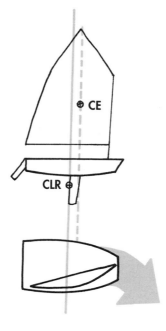

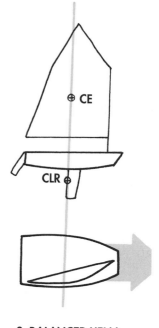

1. WINDWARD HELM
Center of Effort Aft/Leeward of Center of Lateral Resistance

Correcting Windward Helm
• move rake forward
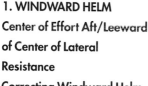
• hike harder
• depower sail
• raise daggerboard
• move weight aft

2. LEEWARD HELM
Center of Effort Forward/Windward of Center of Lateral Resistance

Correcting Leeward Helm
• move rake aft
• move more to leeward
• power up sail
• lower daggerboard
• move weight forward

3. BALANCED HELM
CE and CLR line up

CE = Center of Effort
CL = Center of Lateral Resistance

a little. If you luff immediately, then ease your sail and depower a bit. Also try raking the mast forward slightly.

If you feel a strong **leeward helm** (forces on your boat to sail away from the wind), maybe you are heeled too much to windward. Adjust your weight and see if that helps. Also try raking the mast back slightly.

Your daggerboard makes a big difference in performance sailing to windward.

If there were no blade under the water, the force of the wind would just push your boat sideways. But the counteracting force of the wind on the sail and the opposing force of the daggerboard against the water are what work to squeeze your boat forward. This is known as **lateral resistance**.

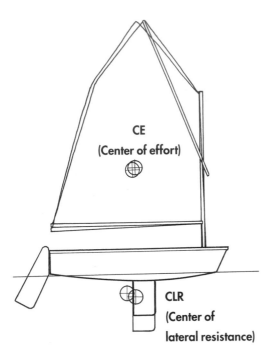

CE
(Center of effort)

CLR
(Center of
lateral resistance)

The center of lateral resistance (CLR) of the underwater surfaces can be changed by moving the daggerboard or by moving your body weight fore and aft. The center of effort (CE) of the sails can be changed by altering the rake, the power of the sail, the heel of the boat, and the trim of the sail.

Raising the daggerboard a little will reduce your helm and your angle of heel by making the area of the underwater resistance smaller. Small sailors will benefit from raising the centerboard a little bit in heavy air.

Sailing on a Reach

Reaching is the fastest point of sailing. You are sailing with the wind coming over the side of the boat, giving your sail its most direct hit. Your boat will really scream along if the water is flat and smooth.

But just as the wind is hitting your boat side-on, so are the waves. So if it is choppy or you're sailing in the ocean, you must pay attention to trying to steer a straight course.

You might have to steer either above or below your target to keep from losing speed by excessive rolling.

Keep your daggerboard about halfway down on a reach. Too far up, and you will blow sideways. Too far down, and you will heel too much.

You want your sprit eased off just enough so that you can see the beginnings of a wrinkle between the head and the clew. This will give your sail a fuller, more wind-catching shape.

Sailing on a Run

Sailing with the wind, or running free, is one of the highlights of sailing. There is an old sailors' saying, meaning the very best of luck: "May the wind be always at your back." This is a welcome point of sail, especially after a hard beat to windward.

6341 heels to windward on this run to balance the helm (note how the tiller is exactly in the center), as well as to get the sail higher and minimize the amount of the hull in the water.

As you bear away from the wind by pulling the tiller toward you, you will feel the wind swing your stern. Let your mainsheet out until the boom is perpendicular to the boat. You want your boat to remain stable downwind, heeled to windward.

Your boat should heel to windward as the wind pushes from astern. Even the waves are helping to push you in this direction. They will add to your speed as they move under you.

Optimists are notorious for bow plowing and swamping when running. Once your bow pushes into the water, you will need to pump your sail once with some force, pulling in three feet or so of mainsheet, then easing it out. Also pay attention to your weight and be ready to slide back when you get a puff.

As in sailing to windward, be ready to counterbalance any slowing-down effects of the waves.

Sit a little farther back in the boat to keep your bow up in a good breeze, but move forward as you feel the stern start to drag. In a light breeze, you want to keep your weight forward. It's all about keeping as little of the hull in the water, presenting as little resistance to the waves as possible. The best sailors constantly adjust their weight to keep the boat at the fastest angle of heel. The angle of heel is our most important reference. When you are sailing fast relative to other boats around you, note how much your boat is heeling and then try to keep sailing at that angle.

Keep the sail out and filled. A heel to windward will keep your sail high, over the hull instead of over the water, and able to catch more wind. This is called kiting.

You need your vang on tightly when

Heeling to windward when sailing downwind balances the rudder, gets the sail up higher, and reduces friction with the water.

you are sailing off the wind. This keeps your boom down and your sail shaped to collect the wind better.

Your daggerboard can be up until you have 3 cm sticking out the bottom on a run, but if you feel the boat rolling too much from side to side, put the daggerboard down a little to add control.

Look at your masthead fly to make sure you aren't sailing by the lee (with the wind coming over your leeward quarter). You don't want a surprise jibe. You're not really using the power of the wind most efficiently if you sail by the lee.

Your wind pennant at the top of your mast will give you a good indication of this. If it starts to point on the other side from the sail, head up a little (push your tiller toward the sail, then straighten back out).

Be ready to shift your weight on a run. You are sitting back in the boat to keep the bow from smashing into waves and stopping the boat, and you are also trying to maintain a windward heel.

Because you are keeping the boat heeled to windward to keep the sail over the hull, you are susceptible to, and want to prevent, drastic rolls, especially to windward. If you start to feel a big roll

In light wind, move your
weight forward to get the
transom out of the water.

Planing

Planing is skimming on the surface of
the water at a high speed.

Getting an Optimist up on a plane
takes a pretty strong breeze, but what a
thrill it is! The full force of the wind and
the full power of the wave shoots the boat
right along.

To take advantage of a plane, plan for
it. You need to be on a course that allows
you to sail a little higher than dead
downwind, so that you have the ability to
bear off in a puff.

When you feel the puff about to hit,
get your weight well out and head down
with it. If it's a big puff, you may have to
extend your arm to ease the mainsheet
out a little to keep the boat from heeling
too much. You want the wind and the
wave to be pushing as flat a hull as you
can balance it to be.

As the wave catches the boat, it will
raise the stern. Get ready for a big push.
You have to keep the boat on the wave as

coming on, tug your mainsheet quickly to
change the air flow. Just a sharp pull, then
back to where you once had it.

Lean in fast if you start to roll to
windward. Lean out fast if you start to
roll to leeward. Sit on the rail and face
forward. Keep your mainsheet arm
working: flex at the elbow to bring in the
sail, extend your arm to ease it out.
Heading up will also reduce rolling.

Too far aft! Note how far the
bow is out of the water. This
means that the stern is
dragging through the water,
slowing down the boat.

long as possible, so don't let the bow plow. Sit well back, and out as far as you need to for balance. Don't let the boat roll! Keep it as flat as possible.

But you don't want the wave to pass without taking the boat with it, so as you feel the wave under you, shift your weight forward a little to keep the bow from lifting, and slide right along with the wave. You need to keep your speed up, so work the mainsheet as well.

Look ahead of you. If you are sailing in a strong breeze in big waves, you want to make sure your bow doesn't just slam into the wave ahead. Shift your weight to prevent this, and try heading up a bit as you come off one wave and onto another. This will keep your boat speed up, even between waves. Remember to head back down again as soon as you can so you don't get too far off course.

To accelerate on a plane or when you are surfing, give your speed an extra boost by reaching in the boat and yanking in the mainsheet really fast. Hike out again quickly. You can do this legally as long as it is not a repeated motion, and you aren't using it as a tactic to roll the boat to windward.

Remember that when you trim your mainsheet, your boat will want to round up into the wind. Be firm with tiller control.

Things to Avoid Downwind

PITCH-POLING

Caused by your bow smashing into a wave with such force that it stops the hull. The sail, rig, and you, unfortunately, keep going. Think of it as a really bad example of a cartwheel.

You can control this by making sure your boat is as dry as possible downwind, and that you are paying attention to shifting your weight aft as the boat sails up and over waves. If you are out of control, simply sail a higher course. Avoid sailing by the lee.

BROACHING

This is an out-of-control maneuver. No one chooses to broach. It happens when you start to jibe, intentionally or not, and

To avoid pitch-poling, keep your weight aft and steer a higher course when riding a wave.

you lose control. Too much heel, and the boat thinks it is being steered by the side of the boat in the water, not the rudder, so it whams back onto the previous jibe. This can result in a knockdown, swamping, or capsizing.

Tacking

In order to maintain steerage, you want to tack as quickly and as smoothly as possible. You want to get through the wind and onto the other tack as fast as possible, but without losing much speed. Only tack when you are prepared and your boat is sailing at top speed. If you make your tack when you are moving fast you lose less distance during the maneuver.

This does not mean that you can tack from a reach by just slamming your tiller over.

As you head up into the wind, pull in your mainsheet. This will speed your turn into the wind, so make your tiller adjustments minimal. Go slowly as you approach the wind, then as you start to turn through it, push your tiller toward the sail quickly and definitely.

When you are on the other tack (the sail has crossed the boat and is filling), straighten your tiller out smoothly to the center of the boat.

You have to get across your boat, too, and because your weight is so critical to the movement of the Optimist, you want to do this in synch with the boat.

Shift sides as soon as the sail has crossed the boat. Be ready. Do this in one (or as few as possible) step. Keep your weight on your feet when maneuvering.

You should hold the tiller or hiking stick behind you as you switch sides, but as soon as you have tacked and are seated, switch hands and move the tiller or hiking stick in front of you! Don't try to steer with it behind your back longer than you need to to maintain a new course. Change hands quickly.

You need to power your boat through a tack. Don't be afraid to make definite steering adjustments, but keep them as smooth and as controlled as possible.

And then there is **roll tacking.**

Roll tacking allows you to keep your momentum up, and helps prevent getting stuck in irons. This is the preferred way to get your Optimist from one tack to the other.

When you decide to tack, make sure you are up to speed. Head off a little to gain more, if you need the power. Keep the boat flat.

You should only need to push the tiller toward the sail about a quarter of the way across to get your bow through the wind. As you push the tiller toward the sail, stay where you are. When the bow has gone through the wind, the boom has crossed the boat, and the sail is on the new tack, jump to the new windward side. Keep

To roll-tack, trim your main in as you round up toward the wind. Change sides when the boat is head to wind.

facing forward, and as you adjust to your new course, exchange hands for the tiller and main. Use your centerboard trunk to vault yourself across if necessary.

What you have done is to roll your boat smoothly onto a new tack. This means that your luffing sail has not disturbed the forward momentum of the hull. You have gone from sailing flat on one tack to flat on the other tack, without bobbing and crashing about in between.

Another way to roll-tack your boat is to take a more aggressive attitude about rolling the boat.

As you start your tack (as the bow starts to come through the wind and your sail starts to luff), *really* roll the boat to what was windward (that's where you still are). Slide your weight out (butt over rail) and stay there until the boat heels over and the boom switches sides.

Keep your weight on your feet. Use the sail to help you steer.

Then *jump* to the other side, with your knees facing forward, so you are going in the direction you want the boat to be going. Sort of as if you were jumping a skateboard. Remember, you always want to be moving the boat ahead.

Make sure you jump across the boat and not too far aft. That will drag your stern and slow you down.

Don't switch hands until you are sitting on the new windward side and the boat is sailing the new course.

You will be steering with smooth movements here. This is not the time to be yanking or jerking the hiking stick.

Your boom bridle should be held high enough not to catch on you or your life jacket during even the most athletic tack. Make sure the mainsheet snap shackle is snag-free.

Jibing

When you jibe, you use the same principles as when you tack, except your stern turns through the wind, not your bow.

Think about the edges of your sail. When you tack (come about), the luff edge passes through the wind first. It's a stiff, straight edge, since it's attached to the mast. Not so when you jibe! The full, floppy length of the leech must pass through the wind first. This makes a jibe less controlled than a tack, and you need to be prepared.

And you need to help more, getting the stern of the boat through the wind.

Make sure your daggerboard isn't sticking up so much that it will interfere with the boom as it crosses the boat. But don't jam the board too far down or the boat will "trip" over it.

This happens when you try to turn too tight a corner with too much blade digging into the water as the boat is moving sideways. Your boat sort of gets caught, and you will tip (maybe over) to leeward. Just straighten your tiller and balance the boat.

As you start to pull the tiller away from the sail, put your stern through the wind, sheet in a little, just to take up any slack.

Grab all the mainsheet parts and fling the boom over your head as you are still turning.

Again, this is not a time for huge tiller movement. Stay smooth and controlled.

As your sail switches sides, ease the mainsheet a little to absorb the shock of the jibe. *Jump* to the new windward side and straighten your tiller.

Keep your balance and keep the boat balanced during a jibe.

The key to a successful jibe is switching hands at the right instant. For a split second you should hold both the mainsheet and hiking stick in one hand.

UNEXPECTED OR FLYING JIBE

You are running before the wind, when all of a sudden your boat feels strangely light, the sail doesn't look quite full, and then—*wham!*—the boom crashes all the way over the boat to the other side. You may find out why it's called a "boom."

This is not good.

Watch your masthead fly/wind pennant. If you seem to be sailing by the lee, push your tiller away toward the sail and head up a little. Keep the wind over your windward quarter, and this won't happen.

THE S JIBE

This technique should be used when it is blowing hard and there is a chance of capsizing. Use extreme care, being especially watchful for high seas and sudden gusts. You control the jibe by steering your boat through an S pattern while maneuvering. In an Optimist, you should have slightly more than one half of the board down when jibing, which will stop your boat from spinning out yet keep it from tripping over itself. The trick is to keep the boat under the top of the mast.

The S jibe, step by step: On course; bear down; by the lee, bring sail over; as sail is coming over, steer back in the direction the sail is going (this takes the pressure off the sail); once the sail is on the new side, stay by the lee until under control; come up onto course when completely under control.

THE ROLL JIBE

Roll jibing should be used whenever possible. The big advantage of this technique is that you jibe the boat without changing course and can accelerate rapidly.

Basically, you are sailing dead downwind or slightly by the lee. Roll the boat to leeward about 10 degrees, then roll it hard to windward, giving a rapid trim on the mainsheet and throwing the boom over. When the sail is just reaching

To execute an S jibe, steer in the direction of the mainsail as it crosses the centerline of the boat to help give you control.

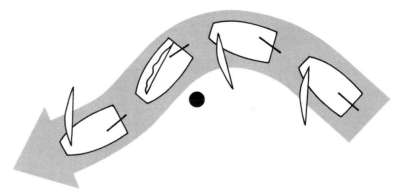

90

the other side, roll the boat back to windward. Again, you are in effect rocking. This takes practice, but you will find that you will accelerate fast. As conditions become windier, you will have to adjust your technique.

Meeting an Obstruction

It is a bad idea to hit anything, ever, with your boat. Keep your eyes open, scan the waters around you, and you can probably avoid all obstacles.

If one appears and you need to get away from it fast, just remember that you turn your tiller toward the obstacle to go away from it. "Tiller Toward Trouble" is the Optimist slogan.

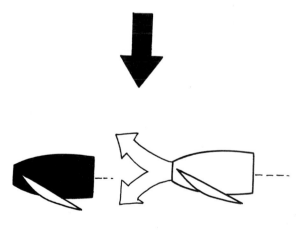

Same tack; black is clear ahead so white must stay clear.

Capsizing

It happens to everyone. "If you don't capsize once a season, you're not really trying," said one famous racing skipper.

But capsizing takes up valuable racing time, and while it is sometimes unavoidable, good boat handling and focus can help you stay upright and racing, instead of enjoying an unplanned bath.

PREVENTING A CAPSIZE

There are signs that you might be about to capsize. If you recognize them early, you can usually prevent a swim.

If your boat starts to capsize to windward, which can happen if a strong wind puff suddenly stops, just lean into your boat to balance it. Don't be afraid to hop off the rail if it's a very sudden wind change. Pulling in your mainsheet or heading down quickly can also help.

If your boat starts to go over to leeward, let your mainsheet out and head into the wind (by pushing the tiller toward the sail). You will luff, and your boat should straighten up.

Tipping your boat over might seem scary, but it's not. And sometimes capsizing your boat might seem like just the thing to do on a hot summer day.

Of course you want to try very hard *not* to capsize. If you are racing, it means spending time righting and bailing your boat, time you could be sailing to your marks.

Righting your boat. It is best
to pull the boat up into the
safety position first.

But capsizing an Optimist just happens sometimes, if you are trying really hard to take advantage of the wind.

First, always remember the golden rule: *stay with your boat.* If you do need someone to help you, it's easier and safer if you are close to your boat. The beach may look plenty close enough, but chances are it's farther away than you think. Righting the boat is a quicker way to get to shore.

But if you end up in the drink, righting the boat is easy.

Swim up to the hull and put your daggerboard all the way down. Of course, if your hull is upside down, the daggerboard will be pointing up. You'll need it for a hand-hold.

Grab the end of the daggerboard with both hands and brace your feet on the side of the boat. Now use your weight to pull the sail up onto the water.

Swim to the bow and let the boat turn into the wind. Once into the wind, swim to the side and grab on to the daggerboard. Then, holding on to the side of the boat, pull it right up. Your sails will be luffing because your boat is pointing into the wind. It is best if you are able to bring the boat up in the safety position with the boom off to the side.

Still holding on to the sides, slide astern a little and grab your hiking straps so you can pull yourself into the boat. Then bail, bail, bail!

If you think you have too much water

If you capsize, take your time. This sailor is glad to be wearing his life jacket.

still in the boat after you have gotten it upright, and if the water isn't too cold, you can always tip the boat over and try to let more water drain out when it's lying on its side, before you stand on the daggerboard and bring the sail out of the water.

Remember that the Optimist has air bags to keep it afloat, and if you let them bring the boat at least halfway out of the water, then you'll have less to bail once you get in.

Or you can try shaking the hull when it's lying on its side in the water before you quickly step on the daggerboard.

Basic Rules of the Road

There are rules and laws that car drivers must obey. They help organize and control traffic on the roads.

On the water, there are also "laws," or Rules of the Road, but there isn't a sailing policeman to enforce them. The penalty for breaking the laws on the water isn't getting a ticket. Usually, it's having to pay for the damage to the other boat if you were in the wrong. And it can take a lot of allowances to repair someone else's broken boat.

So it is practical, and makes sailing more pleasant for everyone, if you understand the way traffic is controlled on the water. Learn and obey the rules of the waves.

These rules get a little more complicated when you are racing, but there are some basic rules for you to know even the very first time you go for a sail.

STARBOARD TACK HAS RIGHT-OF-WAY

This means that if you are sailing on the starboard tack, a boat on the port tack has to move for you. If you are the port-tack boat, you must stay clear. If you don't, then you are at fault.

Port　　　　　　**Starboard**

When boats are on opposite tacks, the boat on port tack must keep clear.

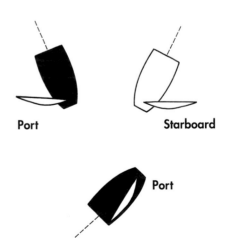

Port　　　　　　**Starboard**

Port

When a starboard-tack boat is on a run, it still has right-of-way over any port-tack boat, even one sailing close hauled.

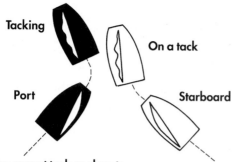

Tacking

On a tack

Port

Starboard

You cannot tack so close to another boat that there is a collision or that the other boat has to change its course to avoid a collision while you are still tacking. The same rule applies to jibing too close.

Since these boats are on the same tack and overlapped, the windward boat (the one on the other's windward side) must keep clear.

W

L

Even though the wind is coming over these boats' transoms, the windward boat must keep clear. Remember, windward and leeward sides are determined by where the boom is (leeward side).

W

L

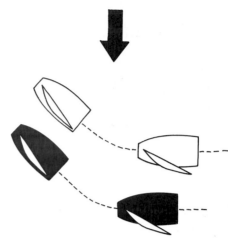

Same tack; black is the leeward boat and may luff as she pleases. White, as the windward boat, must keep clear.

TACKING (OR JIBING) BOAT MUST STAY CLEAR

This means that you can't change direction and slam right into a boat that is sailing along near you. You have to wait until you won't hit before you change direction.

SAME TACK—OVERLAPPED

The leeward boat has right-of-way. This means that the boat on the other's leeward side has right-of-way and the boat more to windward has to keep clear.

SAME TACK—NOT OVERLAPPED

The boat clear ahead has right-of-way. This means that the boat catching up from behind has to stay clear.

POWERBOATS MUST STAY CLEAR OF SAILBOATS

But don't push this one! If a big tanker is motoring along, sail away! You can change course much faster than the tanker can. The same is true for most powerboats.

Rules of the Road dictate that a sailboat not force a ship out of the channel in confined waters. This is serious. Stay clear.

Most big ships make big waves as they move through the water (this is called their **wake**), and a little Optimist can be swamped by the wake of a not very big powerboat!

Even though you are under sail, stay clear of large vessels with limited maneuvering room in channels.

Other Rules and Tips

Big ships make walls against the wind. If you put a big boat between you and the wind, you will lose your wind power and stop. This is dangerous, because you want to be able to steer your boat at all times. You need wind power! Don't lose it in the shadow of a big boat!

Sailboats cannot interfere with fishing boats. If you see lines out, or net floats, sail away from them.

When you know the Rules of the Road, you also need to know that it's all right to break one of the Rules Ashore. You must make sure that any boat you think might not be aware of your presence finds out that you are there. YELL!

Yelling is okay. On the water, it's called **hailing,** and it means getting the attention of another vessel. When you know you have the right-of-way, announce it. Don't whisper "starboard tack" as if you were at the symphony. Think ballpark, and your team just hit a home run!

As soon as the other boat acknowledges, and either tacks away or tells you to hold your course, no more yelling, please—unless you think that by holding your course you may still have a collision. Yell once again, but don't wait until just before the crash. If it still looks as if you're going to wreck, change your course. Tack or jibe away. Head down to go under the other boat's stern. Do

whatever you have to to avoid a direct hit. As mentioned earlier, move the tiller toward trouble.

Remember that an Optimist is a small boat and may be impossible to see from a powerboat. No one on the big boat will be able to hear you yelling "RIGHT-OF-WAY!" over the loud engine. Don't take chances. Stay clear!

1940 must thread his way through a capsized boat and a boat hitting the mark. Who has the right-of-way?

Racing

Competition

Once you have mastered the basic technique of sailing an Optimist, you will probably want to test—and improve—your skills by racing. A series of races is called a **regatta,** and regattas can be found at yacht clubs, camps, and community centers in eighty-nine countries. All around the world Optimist sailors can find good competition—and make lasting friends—nearby or on the other side of the globe.

The Optimist dinghy is a beautiful boat to race. It is a safe, stable, basic boat, but it allows for an infinite variety of adjustments to help you sail fast in all wind conditions.

When you race, you will learn more about handling and tuning your boat. You will learn from other sailors, from your own performance, and by comparing notes. You will also become part of a pretty amazing group of sailors. Many Olympians and other top sailors got their start racing Optimists.

Because it wouldn't be fair to make younger sailors race against older, more experienced skippers in the United States, each Optimist skipper is assigned to an age group, called a **fleet.** These fleets are named red, blue, and white. White fleet is for skippers who are ten or under at the time of the regatta. Blue fleet is for skippers who are eleven to twelve. Red fleet is for skippers who are thirteen to fifteen.

Green fleet is a special novice fleet, just for beginners. Green fleeters can be any age up to fifteen. Green fleet is always limited to skippers who are in their first year of racing Optimists.

The fleets simply place the competition into age groups or, in the case of green fleet, a skill group. Fleets keep the competition fair and challenging for everyone. They level the playing field and give skippers of all ages and skills a chance to compete against their peers and to have a fair chance to take home a trophy. The fleets also help sailors judge how they're doing against their peers.

First Race

Before you even launch your boat for a race, there are a few things a good competitor needs to do.

Make sure your sail is tied on properly. This is critical. It may take a couple tries to get it right, but you can do it if you practice.

Make sure your equipment is in good

condition—and that you have it all. Add extras for things that get lost or break.

Check out the weather. Take a look at what other boats on the water are doing. Listen to a weather forecast so you will have an idea of what you can expect on the water.

Put on or take off whatever clothing you need so you will be comfortable, dry, and enjoy our race.

Know what the tide is doing. If tide is a factor, or if there are strong currents, know when and where they flow.

PRESTART PREP

Before you head out to the race course, take a minute to make sure your boat is shipshape. Sail away from the shore or the dock and just luff while you check things out. Watch the best racers. They all do this. Is everything stowed close to the daggerboard so there is no moveable or extra weight in the bow or stern?

Does your sail trim look right? Any adjustments for the wind or seas you need to make to feel comfortable about the way the boat is rigged?

Are *you* comfortable? You don't want to be pestered by a pair of pants that pinch. If you are distracted while you are sailing, you won't be giving the boat full attention.

This quiet minute before a race is important. Incorporate it into your routine!

DAILY OPTIMIST CLASS RULE CHECK

The measurement band in the middle of the sail must be between the bands on the mast at all times.

• The distance between the sail in each grommet and the boom or the mast must not be more than 10 mm (Rules 3.6.11 and 3.6.12). We recommend that the sail never be more than 5 mm.

• The mast must have a system to prevent it from coming out of the mast step (Rule 3.5.2.11).

• The bowline must float and be 8 meters long and 5 mm in diameter. This line must be attached to the hull and tied to the mast step (Rule 4.3.B).

In addition, your boat must have:

• Three air bags that are inflated, with a minimum buoyancy of 90 liters (Rule 3.2.6.1).

• A tie-in line from the daggerboard (2 kg minimum weight) to the hull. This will prevent loss in the event of a capsize (Rule 3.3.3 and Rule 3.3.4).

• A bailer that is tied to the boat (Rule 4.3.A).

• A rudder system that will keep the rudder in place in the event of a capsize (Rule 3.4.5.2). The rudder blade, tiller, and hiking stick should float, and minimum weight is 1.5 kg (Rule 3.4.3).

• The distance between the boom and the bridle shall not be more than 100 mm (Rule 3.5.3.8).

• A life jacket with a whistle attached should be worn at all times.

• A sail must have the IODA royalty button near the tack.

PRERACE WARM-UP

Be sure that you get on the water with enough time to test your tacks before the start. Practice at least four racing tacks and four racing jibes.

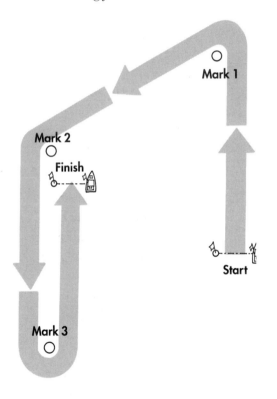

This is a recommended race course for the Optimist dinghy. It is designed to keep boats separated. Most Optimist dinghy races take about forty-five minutes.

Make sure you understand the race course. Decide on the favored side of the course. This side of the course usually has more wind, or less current, or a favorable windshift anticipated. The reason for choosing this side of the course is to help you arrive at the turning mark sooner than your competition.

Imagine the race course as if you were looking down on it from a blimp.

Insert an imaginary wind arrow. Add information about current and tide changes, and think about how that will work for or against you on each leg. Know where you want to be on each leg. If you want, draw the course out on paper, incorporating the wind and current, before you leave.

Sail along with another competitor and compare speed.

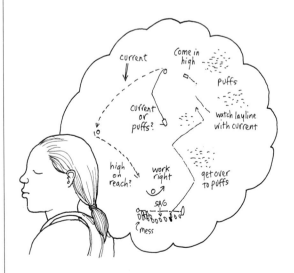

Thinking out course in advance

You can organize a "buddy system" for testing a starting line. You and another boat start at the same time from opposite ends of the starting line. Sail straight tacks until you cross. Keep sailing on for exactly one minute. Use your stopwatch. Tack. You will cross again. Who did better? Keep sailing straight on for exactly one more minute. Tack. Again

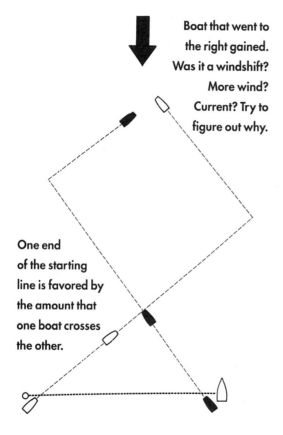

Boat that went to the right gained. Was it a windshift? More wind? Current? Try to figure out why.

One end of the starting line is favored by the amount that one boat crosses the other.

Use the buddy system before the start to see which end of the starting line is favored and which side of the course might be favored.

you cross. By now, you will be able to see which side of the course is favored. It doesn't take long, but it's a little hard to do if the starting line is jam-crammed with boats.

Fast Starts

The most exciting part of a sailboat race for most sailors is the start. It is here that all competitors still have an equal chance, and anticipation of the drive for the line gets the adrenaline pumping. In this game, everyone is a winner. However, at the gun it is those who have planned ahead who pop into the lead.

There are several ways to figure out which end of the line is favored (closer to the windward mark). The first is to luff into the wind. The end that your bow points toward is usually favored. The second is to reach down the line in one direction and then jibe and head in the other direction. Your sail trim will tell you which end of the line is favored. If, for example, you sail luffs on the port tack, the starboard end will be favored.

Starting in a big fleet takes careful practice, but by following a few rules you should be consistently sailing in clear air near the favored end of the line and have the ability to pass at your choosing and not be forced away.

The most important factor is to maintain maximum boat speed when

Figuring out which end of the line is favored

Shoot head to wind in the middle of the line. Your bow will be aimed at the favored end. Sight aross the side of the boat to see how much an end is favored.

Shoot head to wind outside the pin end. Use the side of the boat to sight through the pin toward the committee boat end. The distance away from the boat is the distance that end is favored.

Using sail trim: Reach straight down the line, trimming your sail perfectly. Keep the mainsheet in the same spot and tack or jibe around. If the sail luffs, the end you are aiming at is favored.

Using a compass: Get a compass heading for the starting line. Calculate the angle perpendicular to the line. Do a wind check. The difference from the perpendicular tells you how many degrees one end is favored.

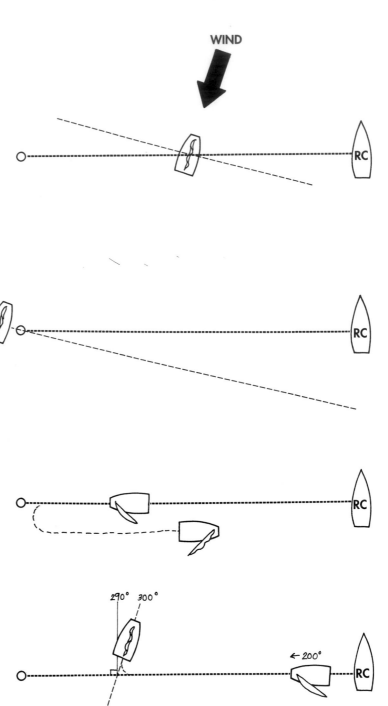

As the start nears, it is important to set up in a good position. Too close to the line and you may get pushed over. Too far away from the line and you may be late and sailing in bad air. With over one minute to the start (blue shape still up on race committee boat), can you find any boats that might be setting up too close to the line? Which boats have a nice hole to leeward?

maneuvering on the starting line. When moving fast you can maneuver easily, but when stopped you have no ability to steer. Making your approach to the line, use the starting line itself as a reference. If you have reached away from the line for one minute you know it will take about one minute to return. Always be aware of where the line is. Use range marks ashore to get an accurate fix on the line.

Try to time the line so you will know how long it takes to sail from boat to pin—leave yourself enough time to start where you want!

When the port end of the starting line is favored, I find that a group of boats will invariably sail down the line, each rounding up under the lee of another boat. In this case, a port approach start

"X" flag—Individual Recall
• accompanied by one sound signal at start
• means the race committee has identified individual boat(s) over early. They willl be scored as premature starters (PMS) unless they return to start properly.

"I" Flag—Round-the-Ends Rule
• will be displayed at or before preparatory signal
• means that any boat on the course side of the start line or its extensions during the final minute must go around an end before starting.

"Z" Flag—20 Percent Penalty
• will be displayed at or before preparatory signal
• means that any boat sailing in the triangle during the final minute will be penalized by the addition of points (equal to 20 percent of the fleet) to your finish position.

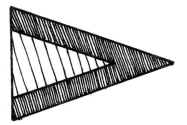

1st Substitute—General Recall
• accompanied by two guns or sound signals at start
• means too many boats are over early for the race committee to identify. There will be a new preparatory signal made one minute after 1st substitute is lowered with sound signal.

Black Flag—Disqualification Flag
• will be displayed at or before preparatory signal
• means that any boat sailing in the triangle formed by the ends of the start line and the first mark during the final minute will be scored disqualified (DSQ), even if that start resulted in a general recall.

Fifteen seconds to go. 5810 is running out of room! Note the sag in the middle of the line.

Five seconds to go. 5810 puts it into park. 6244 is in trouble. Can 6246 hold back?

Zero—the start! Hey, where did 2773 come from? It's smoking but over early! 5810 is sitting on the mark *and* over early. 6244 is shooting ahead to wind just behind the mark.

Plus-two seconds. 2773 begins to bear off to restart. 5810 is still sitting on the mark—ouch! 6244 is starting to go backwards in irons. . . .

Question: What does 5810 have to do to continue in the race?
Answer: Perform a 360 for hitting the mark and restart by sailing below the line or around the end.

might be effective as long as you tack onto starboard at least one minute before the gun. If the line is too crowded for this kind of maneuver, the only solution is to join your competitors.

However, you can get off the line faster by following several rules:

1. While your sail is luffing, always keep your boat on the course that you are going to be sailing. If your boat is in the no-go zone (pointing directly into the wind), it takes a long time to turn the boat before accelerating.

2. Rock the boat to windward to fill your sail and accelerate.

3. Always keep as much or more speed than your competitors when approaching the line. Never allow yourself to go slower.

4. Keep sheet adjustments slacked off so you can gain extra speed by trimming.

5. When the fleet begins trimming for the start, always, always be the first boat to trim in for the start.

6. Always accelerate as you approach the line; never slow down.

If you are approaching the start on starboard and you notice a port tacker is attempting to tack underneath you, it helps to bear off and sail right at the boat, being as intimidating as possible. Even hail "starboard" to prevent this boat from tacking in this situation. It would be best for them to sail on beyond you.

If you are luffing for the line and there are a number of boats around you, the simple rule is to close the distance with boats to windward of you and to open the distance with the boats to leeward.

If there is a boat to windward, you want their bow at your stern quarter. If there is a boat to leeward, try to maintain a position with the boats bow to bow. Never allow yourself to sit on a leeward boat's windward quarter. You will never be able to accelerate for speed.

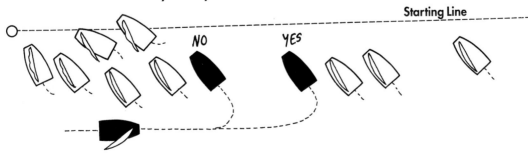

Go beyond this mess! It's too crowded and they're early.

Tack into this hole so you have room to leeward to accelerate in.

Starting Line

NO

YES

Starting in Light Wind

Starting in light wind takes finesse and concentration. Here are several techniques.

1. During the prestart, always stay on the starting line.

2. During the entire prestart maneuver, make the boat sail as fast as possible. Remember, the faster you maneuver the faster the boat stops, so make your maneuvers deliberate and slow.

3. Make a decision on which side of the course you are going to head for well before the start. Look for every sign available of favorable current and wind. The best source is often boats tuning up.

4. There is often more wind one hundred yards to windward of the starting line. By being the first to this new breeze you will gain a substantial new edge.

5. When making your final approach to the line, head directly at a boat approaching you on port so they are forced to maneuver out of your way. If there is a boat to leeward, slow down early and let them sail away. Do not wait until the last moment.

6. Concentrate on speed and you will pop away from the fleet.

Determining Where to Start

Break the line into thirds. Remember, only one boat is going to win an end, so play it safe and get a good start near the favored end. Remember, you can determine the favored end of the line by luffing into the wind at the middle of the line. The end of the line that the bow points toward is favored.

If most of the fleet is stacked at the leeward end, it may be better to plan your start for about one-third of the way up from the leeward end to avoid the crowd.

Where you start is also determined by

Pin end
Port end
Leeward end
Left end

Midline

Boat end
Starboard end
Windward end
Right end

what side of the course you want to be on. Determine the velocity of wind on both sides of the course. A good way to do this is to get together with another boat before the start and sail off on opposite tacks. After one minute of sailing, tack back together again. Assuming that both boats are sailing at the same speed, you can determine which side of the course is favored. If you have time, use three boats. Have two go off on opposite tacks for five to ten minutes and the third tack up the middle of the course every two minutes.

With three boats, you will be able to determine whether the port, middle, or starboard side of the course has more wind. By sailing the leg in advance, you can predict what will happen during the race.

The current will determine where you want to start. If the current is sweeping you into the committee boat or one of the starting buoys, you will want to be on a tack so that you are set away from the obstruction. Remember that it is important to note the current.

Study the action of the water on the turning marks. You can tell the direction (set) and speed (drift) of the current by taking bearings on the anchored buoy or boat.

When in doubt, stay up current.

Port-Tack Start

You should use the port-tack approach about 50 percent of the time. It works best at the leeward end, but can be very effective anywhere along the line. When using the port approach, you must keep constant track of time and must know exactly where you are in relation to the line and other boats. Make sure that you are the last boat running down the line and that you are the last boat to jibe onto port tack. If the fleet seems late, note your time as you pass the leeward end of the line and run the time down the line, allowing time for a tack and then a tack for the line. If the fleet is early, sail past the first group of boats and tack through the first hole. There are several things to keep in mind: Remember that you are on port tack; remember that you have to judge whether or not the fleet is going to be early so that you can get past the first pack of boats and still have time to tack and get up to the line. Many sailors will sit on the line during the last one to two minutes before the start and often they will open a good-sized hole to leeward so that you can sail right up to them and tack, getting a safe leeward for yourself while they are left in bad air. The port-tack approach is the easiest starting technique to master and should be used at least once each practice day.

The port (buoy) end of this start line is very favored. 5386 and 10 are attempting port-tack starts. 2773 on starboard may cause a problem.

At the gun, 2773 tacks and 5386 is able to sail through without fouling. 10 is not so lucky and must wait for the starboard boats to pass. Note how many boats are at this end of the line and how far below the line many are.

The lead four boats are off on port! 10 is still looking for a path, but will have a better start than most of the fleet because the pin end is so favored.

Dip Start

The dip-start technique should be used when the current is running through the line or when it is difficult to cross the line on starboard tack. Often used at Opti regattas, the "one-minute rule" forbids the use of the dip start, since after a general recall you are not allowed over the starting line within one minute before the start. If you do go over the line, you must round either end before starting. We don't recommend using the dip-start technique often because your competitors can easily use their leeward advantage to prevent you from getting down to the line.

In the dip start you wait well above the line, noting the position of the fleet. You will be able to see a hole opening up. Allowing just the amount of time needed, reach down to the line and round up with a lot of speed below the line as the gun goes off. Don't let yourself get too far down the line so that you have to head dead downwind to get to the line. You have a lot more speed on a reach.

When you round up, keep your boat flat so that you don't go sideways, especially if there is a boat to leeward of you. You will be able to round up easier if you keep three-quarters of your board down instead of full board because the boat won't trip over itself. As you round up, trim your sails slowly to maintain your speed. The faster you round up, the faster you will slow down. Practice this start several times a week. You may not get the opportunity to use it often, but when you do it could mean the difference in your standing if you do it well. Remember: round slowly to maintain speed; three-quarters board; trim slowly, but don't luff; keep your boat flat.

If you see a competitor about to execute a dip start, stay to leeward of him and don't allow him room to dip below the line. If you do this, keep in mind where you are and the time remaining so that you will still get off the line clearly.

Never pass to leeward of a competitor using the dip start unless you are sure that you can break through his lee into clear air. This is relatively hard in an Optimist.

Barging Start

The barging start is potentially the best start and is actually the last part of a dip start. When using it, however, beware of right-of-way leeward boats.

In the barging start, you reach along the line and come up just before the gun goes off. This can also be used with a timed run. Pick a point on the line and time your sail (on a reach) to that point. Don't get trapped sailing too far down the line.

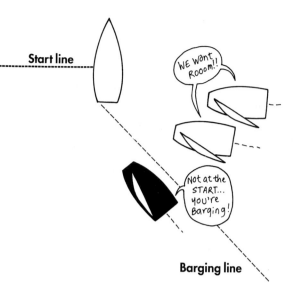

Start line

WE WANT ROOOM!!

Not at the START... you're Barging!

Barging line

THINGS TO REMEMBER ON THE STARTING LINE

1. Never dip beneath someone's stern unless you are sure that you will break through his lee.

2. If you are going to be early, head up to slow down. Do not waste time and distance by bearing off and running down the line.

3. Be careful to avoid collisions. Don't sail around at random. The full time should be used to prepare for your start. Concentrate.

4. If you find you are going to be over early or you are going to be squeezed past either end of the line, bail out early. You will have a better chance of recovery.

5. When running times, you can tell which boats are going to be early and which are going to be late by their positions relative to you and where you are in relation to the line and your time.

Making a good start is one of the highlights of life, and one that pushes a boat to victory.

Starting Line Exits

In every race there is a one-minute window of opportunity to make a fast exit off the starting line that usually determines your position for the rest of the race. There are several key factors to consider during this critical period of time.

1. Sail at full speed at least ten seconds before the gun.

2. Avoid pinching immediately after the start.

3. If you are fading into a leeward boat's bad wind, keep your bow down for fast speed right up to the time you are forced to tack away.

4. Concentrate on when you can make that first tack.

5. When you do tack, don't be afraid to sail behind the sterns of a few boats early in the race.

6. Think speed more than pointing after the start.

7. Only make one tack in the first two minutes of the race.

8. If you are blanketed by several boats and you can't tack away, often being

Here's another start with the pin end heavily favored . . . and 5386 is going for it again! But there is a big wall of starboard boats coming. The boat right by the pin (3946) is early and already bailing out.

Big mess! 5386 is in trouble sitting on port. 3946, which had bailed out, is getting in trouble again. 2064 is early and has nowhere to go but around the pin (note that the starting shape is *not* up on the committee boat).

2064 jibes around to restart. 3946 has nowhere to go and has to tack below the mark. 5386 squeezes in but hits the mark . . . ouch! 4761 is the only *one* that gets a good start at the pin. 3727 started a little ways up the line and tacked to port.

4761 and 3727 are gone! Lots of other boats are still messing around below the pin while any boat with even a decent start is racing upcourse.

You can hardly read the leader's numbers, and look at the mess still by the pin, including 5386, who had dreams of port-tacking the fleet. This can be a risky start, as you can see.

Just like after the start, it is important when sailing upwind to have clear air. Look for "lanes" where you can avoid other boats blocking your wind. Which boat in this photo appears to be sailing in bad air?

patient will pay off because boats ahead of you will eventually tack off your wind.

9. A pre-race tune-up is important so that you will be sailing at full speed. But keep in mind that there is often less wind in the starting area than you will experience later on the course, so you might want to add fullness to your sails for the poststart exit.

10. On very crowded starting lines, it helps to pick a position away from big groups of boats.

Upwind Tactics

Racing to the weather mark is always exciting. Boats are taking different courses to get there. You want to be the one who chooses the right course. You have mapped out your course ahead of time, taking the wind direction, strength, variability, currents, blocking or enhancing qualities of the shoreline, and everything else into consideration. You have planned your strategy to sail within the cone, the area between the ends of the starting line and the mark. You may have to "push the envelope" and sail beyond these lines, depending on the other boats and the wind conditions, but staying within this area should be your target. Keep to your plan, but be flexible. If an unexpected shift comes along, take advantage of it!

Remember the basic strategies of

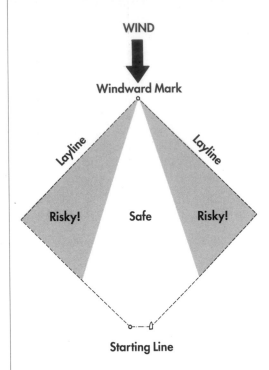

Risk versus safe zone upwind

good upwind Optimist sailing. Keep your boat as flat as possible. Optimists are stable but responsive boats. Body position and sail trim make a big difference.

Right after the start, you want to get your boat going as fast as you can so you can see where you are in the fleet. Don't tack right away unless you know you *absolutely* have to. Remember to sail for the middle of the course at the beginning of the windward leg. No need to take flyers off to one side too early unless you have special knowledge. See if you are gaining or losing distance to windward compared to the boats around you. If you are gaining, keep right on going.

It's important to find clear air right after the start so that you don't get left behind. Here 4812 has tacked and found a lane. 5387 is in bad air and should tack into the clear air "lane."

If you are losing, it's time to think about recovery tactics.

If you are behind (wrong end at the start, slow speed, missed shift, bad air), pick a good time to tack so that you don't have to keep maneuvering to keep clear of starboard-tack boats.

When you have another boat ahead of you giving you bad air, it's best to tack away, but look for a "blocker" first. Wait until a couple other boats have sailed across your stern before you tack. These boats will become "blockers" because they will be leeward and ahead of you. Boats coming along on the other tack will

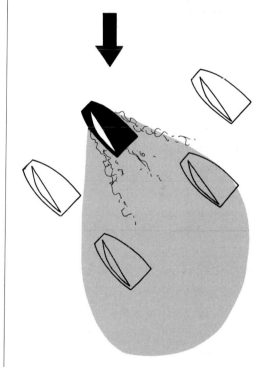

When sailing near another boat, avoid a competitor's wind-shadow.

117

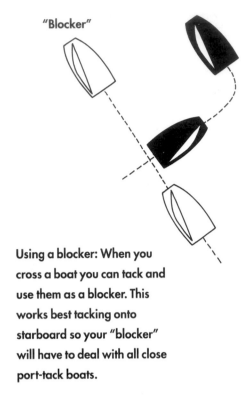

"Blocker"

Using a blocker: When you cross a boat you can tack and use them as a blocker. This works best tacking onto starboard so your "blocker" will have to deal with all close port-tack boats.

have to deal with them, and they will have to tack or suffer disturbed air. That will slow 'em down.

Don't forget that you lose time each time you tack. So if you have blocker boats forcing tacks, and you are sailing in clear air, you're making time!

You want to keep track of what the other boats are doing. Are you sailing as high as the boats on the other side of the course? Are they going faster? Do they have wind you don't?

When you are ahead, watch the competition and stay in between them and the wind, keeping in mind where the mark and the outer edges of the cone are

A double dose of bad air! 70 has a good reason to tack.

so that you don't overstand the mark. When you tack on someone, you either want to protect your position or hurt your competition. Tacking (when and how) is the most important consideration on weather legs. If you are going to tack, you must have a reason: don't just tack for the sake of going about, as this wastes time and distance.

REASONS FOR TACKING

1. You have been headed. (Get into a header at least two boatlengths before you tack so you will stay on the new lifted tack longer.)

2. You are in bad air. (Tack to clear yourself, but be careful that you do not tack into another boat's bad air.)

3. You want to avoid waves. (You want to make a wave parallel to your course. Many times it is better to tack and ride

waves than to smash into them head-on. When you do tack, wait for a flat spot in the waves.)

DIPPING

When you are on port and you have to dip behind a boat on starboard, begin your maneuver early. If you wait too long, you will lose valuable distance by making a sharp alteration of course. Usually four to five boatlengths away is the best time. Your goal should be to have your boat back on a close-hauled course just as the bow of your boat passes below the starboard-tack boat's transom. When you bear off, be sure to ease your sail out to help accelerate for speed.

Dipping

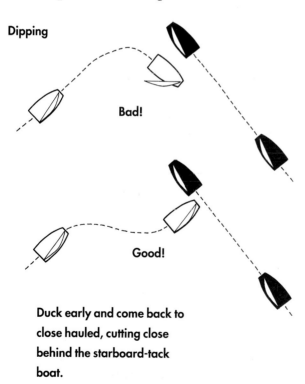

Bad!

Good!

Duck early and come back to close hauled, cutting close behind the starboard-tack boat.

Approaching the Windward Mark

You are sailing for the windward mark with clear air and not too many boats around you. Very nice. Maybe you're even first. Perfect. You can sail your way up the course with little interference and make a smart rounding without worrying about the rest of the fleet.

But what if you are stuck somewhere in the middle of the fleet?

If a large number of boats are trying to fetch the mark at the same time, sail an extra length or two before tacking. You will be able to drive over the top while they are forced to pinch and foul each other. Give yourself room to allow for a lift or blanketing boats.

When making the final tack for the windward mark, overshoot it by one-half to one boatlength if you are within ten overall lengths of the mark. This will help eliminate the chances of not laying the mark because of unfavorable current, a slow tack, a drifting mark, or bad air from another boat tacking on your wind.

If you are clearly making the mark and another boat is crossing your stern, bear off course before he looks your way to see if you are laying the mark. He will then probably continue past the layline, losing distance on you. When you bear off, there are several techniques you can use to convince him that you are not bluffing.

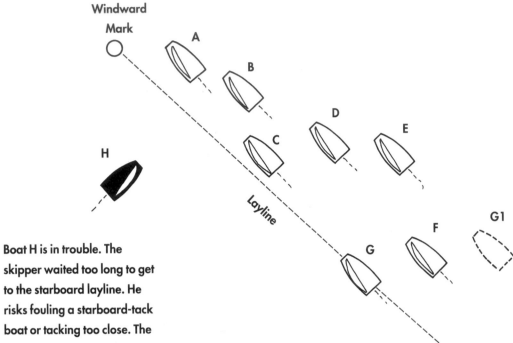

Windward
Mark

A

B

D

E

H

C

Layline

G1

F

G

Boat H is in trouble. The skipper waited too long to get to the starboard layline. He risks fouling a starboard-tack boat or tacking too close. The skipper may find a hole through the "starboard wall" behind C, D, and E. Boat G will have trouble making the mark because of all the bad air and waves. It should have set up in position G1.

Boat 10 doesn't have to give room to the port-tack boat because the "room" rule doesn't count at a windward mark for boats on different tacks. The port-tack boat must keep clear and also may not tack too close to 10.

Keep your sail trimmed in, don't let the boat heel, don't look directly at the other boat, don't make a sudden course change, and wait until he has sailed past you and is looking away before you assume your original course.

On the other hand, if you are not quite making the mark and you want the boat crossing your stern to tack so that he, too, won't make it, head for the mark. Heeling slightly will make you look as though you are pointing higher than you actually are. Appear to be looking at the mark by staring to leeward ahead. Don't let the other skipper see you make any sudden alteration of course. If he falls into your trap and tacks, tack and get up to the layline and tack on your confused

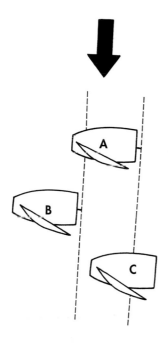

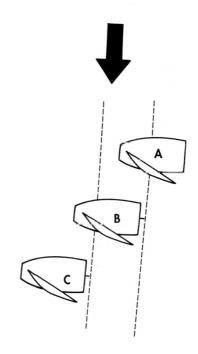

Overlaps are determined by an imaginary line running across the back of the rudder. Any boat in front of that line is overlapped. Any boat not in front of that line is clear astern. Here A is overlapped with both B and C, but C is clear astern of B.

One tricky part of the rules involves a boat in the middle. Even though A and C would not normally be overlapped, the rules say that they are because B is between them and has a overlap on both.

competitor when you are there. If, by chance, he *was* making the mark, he won't now.

THE ROUNDING

Once you have made your approach, start rounding by keeping the boat flat. One rule of thumb is to keep the boat under the mast. This allows you to bear off fast and keeps your boat under control while you increase speed and lose little distance. To keep the boat "under the mast," ease the main out fast. If you let the boat heel, the board will begin to cavitate, allowing air to get between the hull and the water. Your rudder will become ineffective, forcing your boat off balance. Also consider clearing your mainsheet in order to ease it out as you turn. Nothing is slower than an overtrimmed sail downwind.

Any mark rounding is easier and faster with as little course change as possible. The greater the change in course, the

faster your boat will slow down. One way to avoid making major course changes when rounding the windward mark is to slack off slightly before the rounding has begun.

THE GETAWAY

Once the windward mark is rounded, don't delay in making a fast getaway. It is at this point that you head in the direction you want to sail, adjust your sail, and settle in for pure speed. Often, sailors arrive at the windward mark only to relax downwind. This is an opportunity, however, to really get tough and make as much ground as possible. Your getaway sets the stage for your approach to the next mark.

When sailing downwind you may want to loosen your sprit to increase the amount of curvature in your sail. If the sprit is too tight, the sail will create bumps or unnatural curves that will slow you down. Also pull your daggerboard up

5892 already has her daggerboard up for the reach, which helps the boat head off onto the reach and causes less drag underwater. 5805 is just getting its board up, while 5724 is the last one to get its board up even though it is leading.

to reduce friction with the water.

When sailing downwind, keep your weight just aft of the thwart so the bow rides out of the water. The boat sails fastest when the windward hull is tipped to windward. You can judge the correct angle of heel when there is no force steering your boat one way or the other on your tiller. This is a neutral helm. Also heeling to windward allows your sail to fly higher in the air to catch more wind.

The Reaching Leg

On a reach leg, it's a good idea to think about passing boats to windward at the start of the leg, and to leeward at the end of the leg. You always want to try to be inside at the reach mark. If you are outside other boats at the mark, you will have to give them room unless you are able to break the overlap before two boatlengths, but if you are inside, you will own the overlap and will come out of the mark rounding with clear air and a clean lane.

The reach is a perfect opportunity for gaining an advantage by luffing a boat to windward. But make sure your bow is well ahead. Don't luff if you are bow to bow because you will be easily passed. But don't get hung up on this. Throw one definite luff at them. Make it a sharp, serious luff. That ought to give them the message not to try passing you to windward! Threaten to luff anyone who attempts to pass you to windward, but it's bad practice to make the reach leg a continual luffing match. Other boats will sail right by you if you do.

If there are a lot of boats sneaking up behind you, sail a little higher, just to keep your wind clear. If there are a lot of boats ahead of you, sail a bit lower. But always remember to try to sail the straightest reach you can.

Many helmsmen forget where the

Reaching legs can be tricky because you must choose between sailing straight to the next mark (which is the shortest distance) or sailing high to keep your air clear from boats behind you. If the lead boats here (6229 and 2542) get into a luffing duel, 4049 and 6235 could gain by sailing straight to the mark.

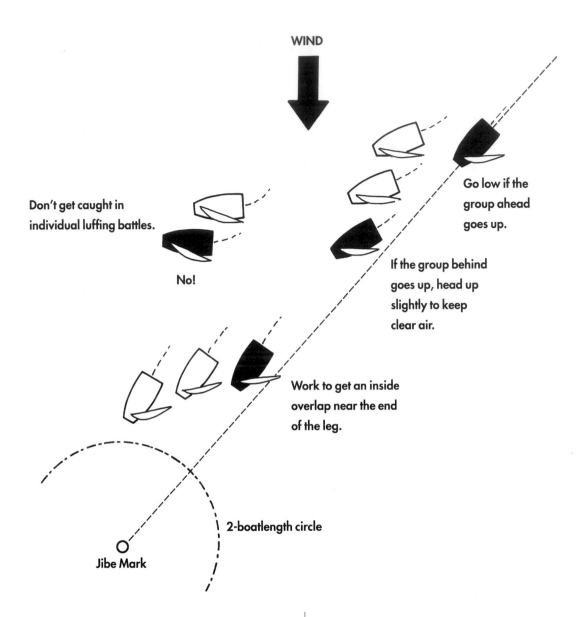

WIND

Don't get caught in individual luffing battles.

No!

Go low if the group ahead goes up.

If the group behind goes up, head up slightly to keep clear air.

Work to get an inside overlap near the end of the leg.

2-boatlength circle

Jibe Mark

mark is located and follow the boats ahead. You must look for the next mark before you make your windward rounding so that you know where to head. When boats ahead of you get into a luffing match, go low to get clear air with a better angle coming into the next mark.

The Run

Going fast with the wind behind you can really be a thrill. Instead of the wind on the sail causing lift, it transfers its energy to directly push your boat along.

Raise your daggerboard when sailing

Which boat has the right-of-way? Which boat must do something to stay clear? Since 2773 is on port tack (boom is to starboard), she must keep clear of 2772, who is on starboard tack. It's okay to cross ahead as long as the starboard-tack boat doesn't have to alter its course to avoid a collision.

straight. The friction of the daggerboard slows the progress of the wind pushing your boat along. Pull it up and you'll see.

DOWNWIND BOATSPEED

Twenty degrees of heel to windward dead downwind keeps the center of effort of the sail over the boat. This technique also reduces the helm on the rudder. Try to keep a neutral helm.

Make sure there is at least 3 cm of daggerboard sticking out of your boat to keep water from getting sucked up into the trunk and slowing you down.

Keep the board all the way up dead downwind. Don't let the boat rock.

Ease your sprit up, and ease your sheet out. Keep your sail just at the edge of luffing by adjusting your mainsheet as necessary—and that might be constantly.

In heavy air, keep weight aft, as aft as you have to; in light air, forward. Stay mobile on the rail so you can move your weight around.

Do not hold on to your daggerboard. You need one hand for the tiller, and one hand to play your mainsheet in and out, for good control in both light and heavy air, and to allow you to "pump" the boat (quickly pulling in the main to straighten up the boat, then easing out the main to return to windward heel).

If you find the boat is out of control downwind, sail a higher course.

Basic rules of thumb: keep air clear; ease sail as far as possible without letting it luff; plan ahead for the next mark and leg; don't let anyone sail over you to windward.

Pull the sheet in if you feel the boat rolling too much to windward. Give the sheet a yank. This is not the time for finesse. If you feel a death roll starting (a really serious tilt to windward), lean in the boat and, again, give the mainsheet a serious trim.

Going downwind, easing the sheet will tip the boat to windward. Sheeting in will heel the boat to leeward. Don't forget this. Use pumping to balance your rig and pop your bow out of a wave.

In light air, you want your sail a little bit ahead of the mast. And make sure your boom vang is on.

As the wind increases, you'll have to keep sheeting the main in. Make sure your vang is on, and tighten it if the wind strengthens.

BOW PLOWING

In addition to side-to-side motion, you have to be aware of fore-and-aft balance as well. You have to pay close attention to where you are in your boat on a run. Sit too far forward, and your boat will plow right into the waves. Sit too far aft, and your tail will drag and slow you down.

Stay mobile on your rail so you can move forward and back as you need to. Your feet should be directly under your windward rail with your weight easily switched to them for scooting back. Sometimes, when the wind blows hard on your sail or you sail into a wave, your bow will want to blow into the wave ahead. To avoid this swamping from the bow first, scoot back and pump your main in two to three feet. This will pop your bow out of the wave and get you surfing.

KEEPING YOUR AIR CLEAR

As you start your run, continue to aim for the mark in as straight a line as possible. Boats behind you will steal your

On a run, you can attack your competition by using your windshadow to slow them down.

wind, so you must be aware of them. You might overtake the boats in front of you, stealing their wind. When another boat's masthead fly is aimed at your sail, your wind will be blanketed.

Pass to windward when you can, but don't get caught in a luffing battle or other boats will pass you by sailing straight to the mark.

Rounding the Leeward Mark

APPROACH

You want to be inside at the leeward mark. This is the only position that will give you clear air when you round. Work your way in, calling for "room at the mark" to boats to leeward you have overlapped, but plan your approach: you also have to give room to anyone inside you!

ROUNDING

Rounding a leeward mark can become a tangle of boats and a racket of noisy skippers. Be smart.

Adjust sail, sprit, etc., for the next leg. Make sure to check the velocity of the wind so that your adjustments are right.

Get adjustments done early if there are many boats around.

If inside at the mark, make a strategical rounding, but only take the room you need, no more.

Try to come in more on a reach than dead downwind. Your speed will be

Room at a mark is determined when the first boat reaches an imaginary circle two boatlengths away from the mark. A boat that is clear astern must keep clear of the boat clear ahead. If two boats are overlapped, the boat on the outside must give the inside boat room to round the mark. The inside boat should take only the room needed, no more.

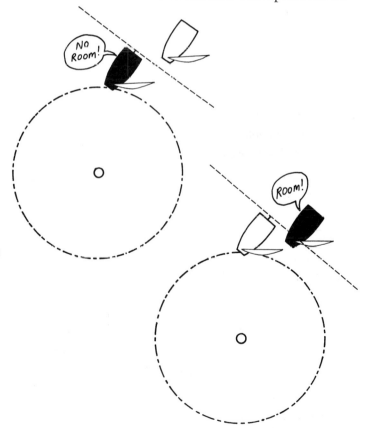

4458 approaches the jibe
mark and executes a perfect
heavy-air S jibe.

Round nice and close at the leeward mark (but be sure not to hit it!) and get onto a close-hauled course right away so you don't waste any distance sailing upwind.

greater and you won't have to round up as much.

Keep the boat flat. If you let it heel, you will lose speed.

Don't get trapped on an inside boat's leeward quarter. Instead, slow down and stay astern, rounding right behind, and try to work up on the windward quarter.

Use any kind of mark, buoy, or channel marker for practice. Execute the mechanical maneuvers of rounding until you have them down perfectly. Once you are able to set up an organized approach, followed by a well-drilled rounding and fast getaway, your mark rounding will be one of your best assets in racing.

GETTING AWAY

After rounding the mark, steer your ideal course for the finish. Avoid spending time worrying about boats immediately behind you, but concentrate on your approach for the finish line or the next mark.

Fast Finishes

In a tight race, as you sprint toward the finish line, your approach can make the difference between victory and defeat.

You have been concentrating on getting ahead of everyone else. But from the last mark rounding, you should also factor in the course that will get you to the finish fastest. So you have to think

6340 crosses the finish line and gets the gun! The finish line is usually between a flag on the committee boat and a buoy.

about all the other boats, *and* how you will cross the line.

Figure out which end of the line is favored. The downwind end, in other words, the end closest to you, is usually favored, but current, wind puffs, and the height of the committee boat (this could block your air) are all factors to consider.

You want to try to cross on starboard tack, but if the port tack is definitely favored, go for it. Same as at the start. Just obey the rules and make your boat go as fast as possible.

It's fine to force a boat to windward of you out past the layline; just remember two things: don't go too far and lose other boats, and don't tack too soon, or your competition will establish an overlap and

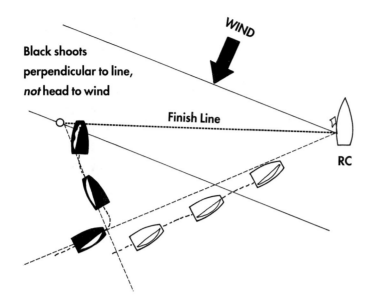

WIND

Black shoots perpendicular to line, *not* head to wind

Finish Line

RC

On an upwind finish, the favored end is the end farthest downwind. If it is unclear which end is closer, sail through the intersection of the laylines to each end to see which is closer. Here, black was slightly behind white, but tacked to the favored end and shot the line (sailed perpendicular to the line) to easily beat white.

call for room at the mark, which you will have to give. This sort of situation is actually fun. There are all sorts of bluffs you can try, but remember that the rules are the law, and you have to obey them.

Dealing with Protests

It's no fun for either party being involved in a protest. Our feeling is that the best policy is to avoid them at all costs—even if it means giving way at times when the rules are on your side. But as long as sailboats race, there will be incidents. Recently the America's Cup made tremendous progress in solving the problem by instituting on-the-water umpires. This system was a big success in San Diego and will certainly continue in the future. For most fleet regattas, there

are no on-the-water umpires so we still have to rely on the testimony of the competitors and the action of the jury.

A boat will protest another boat if there is an infraction in the rules on the race course. The rules are complicated and take a long time to study and understand. But the basic premise is always to prevent boats from having a collision.

Most protests are made when a collision occurs. For example, if you are sailing on port tack and run into a boat on starboard tack, the port-tack boat is obligated to stay clear. Therefore the port-tack boat should make a 720-degree penalty turn. If no penalty turn is made, the starboard-tack boat will protest the port-tack boat and the protest will be heard by a jury. In this case the jury will disqualify or assess penalty points to the boat that was on port and obligated to stay clear.

When you are protested, it is always an emotional shock. Try to make a mental note of the incident and then forget about it for the rest of the race. If you spend the rest of the race worrying about the protest hearing, you will not do well.

Poll your witnesses to understand what happened. Anyone who saw the incident clearly can be used as a witness later.

Over the past fifteen years the U.S. Sailing Association has done a good job certifying judges for competition. The level of competence of juries has improved dramatically. The rules have changed, too, instituting alternative penalties such as a 720 or accepting a percentage penalty when you know you are at fault.

But justice on the water is not automatic. You must work for it. If you are forced into the protest room, either as the protesting yacht or because you are protested yourself, there are a number of key elements to keep in mind to ensure the proper result. After all, if you are right there is no reason to lose protests.

1. Know and study your rules well. The rules change every four years and it helps to go through and read them slowly. I find it best working with another person.

2. Take a few evenings and read the appeals to the rules. There are a lot of great case situations that apply to almost everything that happens out on the water.

3. After the race is over, take a poll of your coach and witnesses to establish precisely what happened on the water. Think in terms of feet and inches, minutes and seconds, degrees of course being sailed, and then write up the situation.

4. Write up your protest neatly and be sure that your diagram is accurate as to the course being sailed and maneuvers by the boats, and that your boatlengths are consistent with the size of the boat and the speed that you are turning.

5. Practice your key points before heading off to the hearing.

6. Be prepared for the other side to throw you a curve. Remember, human nature is such that people tend to see things their own way when they are on another boat.

7. Sailors should respect the other skipper, witnesses, and the protest committee. Different people see things in different ways.

8. Write up all information in outline form. Include all applicable rules and appeals. Use the terminology of the rules in the write-up. Be neat so your protest is easy to understand. Sign form.

9. Insist on your rights under the rules as explained in the International Sailing Federation Racing Rules book. You are entitled to be present at the hearing, cross-examine witnesses, call witnesses, and receive a written decision by the committee.

10. Speak positively and directly to the committee; be firm, cordial, and not angry; explain exactly what happened; use the context of the Rules in your speech; be specific, not vague.

11. Accept the decision of the protest committee. You do have the right to appeal, but an appeal of a decision can only come about if there is a direct question as to the interpretation of the rules. If there is any question as to the facts, an appeal will not be heard. The protest committee must grant permission for an appeal.

12. Pay close attention during the hearing. Often witnesses can be your best ally even if they are not on your side because you can pick up subtle differences in testimony.

Subtle Strategies

It's attention to little details on the race course that makes the difference between winning and losing. Over the past summer I've made a list of little things to do that help.

1. Downwind use a masthead fly to know where your apparent wind is and watch the masthead fly of your competitor to see if he is blocking your wind.

2. If you lose distance after crossing tacks or jibes, have the courage to shift sides of the course.

3. As a rule, always stay on the side of the course where the majority of boats are sailing.

4. When making a maneuver, always know your new course to steer in advance. If you plan a tack or jibe, look at an object on shore or another boat as a reference for your new course.

5. Recovering from adversity is hard to do. But in most races you can make one mistake and still do well in the race. Your goal should be to sail consistently from one race to the next, eliminating little errors along the way.

6. When approaching another boat if you do not have the right-of-way, always accelerate for speed. But this means you must decide early how you are going to meet the other boat. There are two possible maneuvers.

The first is to dip the other boat (you bear off and pass just astern of the right-of-way boat, planning ahead so that you are close hauled and steaming along the second the other boat's stern passes your bow).

The second is to lee-bow the other boat (you sail right up to the other boat's lee bow and quickly tack, sheet in, and power ahead). A good rule of thumb: if you think you could cross the other boat by more than half of a boatlength, then lee-bowing is a good tactic. This is risky business. You must tack quickly and get going quickly.

If you think the crossing would be

closer than that, dip the other boat. Start a dipping maneuver three boatlengths away, but always be aware of the other boat: if it starts a tack to cover you, steer back onto the wind and power up right away.

7. Mistakes to avoid:

• Being over the starting line early.

• Staying in disturbed wind for long periods of time.

• Sailing on the wrong side of the course after you have lost to the boats on the opposite side.

• Getting into a protest.

• Trying to play both sides of the course simultaneously and tacking too often.

• Not bailing out of a bad situation at a mark rounding or on the starting line.

8. When approaching a leeward mark, never allow yourself to sail directly downwind. Always approach the mark on a reaching course.

9. Avoid tacking immediately after a leeward mark so you don't sail back through your disturbed wind and choppy water. We recommend sailing at least three boatlengths.

10. If you are going slowly, make a big change such as easing everything, bearing off for speed or sailing on the other tack.

11. If you are being covered closely by another boat, the time to tack away is when you are faster. Never tack when you are slow.

12. If you are well down in the fleet, don't try to pass every boat at once by taking a flyer. Flyers rarely pay off.

13. Anytime you are making your final approach to the start or a mark, or when you are engaging another boat, it always pays to put your bow down, bear off and accelerate for speed. Sailboats only increase speed when you bear off if you simultaneously ease your sails out. It is

Right after the leeward mark, hull 88 climbs up on the windward "hip" of hull 87, which is now pinned in bad air.

A   B   C

Here's a tricky one! Who has right-of-way and why? Boat A (2767) is on starboard and has right-of-way over the other two, which are on port. Since both B (5021) and C (5491) are on port tack, boat B must stay clear of C because it is the windward boat (closer to the wind).

also important to keep the boat as level as possible when bearing off. If you are heeled over too far, your boat makes leeway and you slow down.

14. Whether you are sailing upwind or downwind, disturbed wind extends about six times the height of the mast, so keep a careful eye on the direction of an opponent's masthead fly. If you are in disturbed wind and within six mast lengths, it is important to take action to keep your wind clear.

15. It pays to review new rules from U.S. Sailing before every major regatta.

16. Over the years I have found that no matter how right you think you are in a protest situation, you only end up winning 50 percent of the time. The best policy is to avoid the protest room at all costs.

17. You often gain valuable information

after the race by talking with competitors. It amazes me how much information you can gather after a day of sailing. People like to talk and you should take advantage of the opportunity.

18. Gary was in a match race that left him from one boatlength in the lead to two boatlengths behind. In frustration Gary announced to the crew, "That's it, this race is over." At which point former NFL football player Larry Mialik stood up, got off the rail and said, "I guess that's it." Of course Gary yelled, "What are you doing?" He returned, "Well, you said the race was over." It was a good reminder that no matter where you are on the race course, the race is never over until you cross the finish line, so keep battling no matter where you are. That attitude will gain valuable points in the long run.

Your Health and Fitness for Sailing

Physical Fitness

While sailing is not usually perceived as a physically taxing sport, any Optimist racer knows that a hard beat to weather, sliding and trimming and balancing and hiking, can be very active, pretty hard work, and very tiring.

While you are on the water, you must remember to prevent sunburn. Wear high-sunblock sunscreen, and a shirt to keep the sun off your back and arms. A baseball hat does nothing to keep the sun off the back of your neck. A hat with a brim all the way around is better.

If you get wet, make an effort to dry off. This isn't always possible when you are racing, but a cold, wet sailor isn't performing at top levels. If you get chilled, go in, especially after a capsize.

You will race better, and handle your boat with more confidence, if you are feeling as healthy and as fit as possible.

By being in good condition and exercising properly, you can increase your stamina. You won't get as tired or as sore as quickly.

It's important that you do exercises the right way. All Optimist sailors are still growing, so it is actually harmful to lift weights, or do weight training.

Aim for aerobic exercise first. Don't just jump right into a big jogging, biking, or swimming program. Start slowly and work your way up.

You do want to strengthen your body. Hiking out for long periods puts a big strain on your legs, knees especially, so work to build strength here.

Knees are really important joints. You don't want to develop knee problems as you get older, so strengthening your leg muscles and paying attention to hiking posture are important.

If you let your bottom sag while you are hiking, you are relaxing a leg muscle that helps support your knee and helps keep it from twisting badly. There is a remedy for this: keep your legs straighter when you hike. This will also help keep your bottom out of the water, and from catching those waves that really slow you down.

Have your hiking straps bungeed above the bottom of the boat and keep them tight. Hook just your toes under the strap, and practice hiking with legs as straight as possible. This becomes more comfortable with practice. You can build a hiking bench to practice on shore.

Limber up before you go sailing. Stretching will help you move better.

Work with a partner to help stretch your muscles.

You also want to be able to move around easily in your boat. You have to, to keep your boat properly balanced and to take advantage of every change in the wind or waves.

So any exercise to keep you limber is good. You want to be able to reach and stretch and twist comfortably.

Sailors who are physically fit feel better, are less likely to get hurt, and have more confidence. It's worth getting in shape and staying in shape.

AEROBIC CONDITIONING

Proper aerobic conditioning can include swimming, jogging, biking, or any exercise that gets your heart rate up and keeps it going. You'll have more stamina and energy if you include some aerobics in your time ashore.

Getting in shape on the hiking bench.

Again, strength training does not include weights for Optimist sailors. Putting too much strain on developing bones and ligaments can cause serious adult malformation and pain. You'll be a cranky, achy adult if you don't pay attention to this.

Rely on circuit training or sports to provide you with increased strength. And remember, the more you sail, the stronger you will be for the tasks you need to accomplish.

Eating Right

How well you eat will help determine how well you sail. Your stomach is definitely a part of you that you must consider when thinking about being physically fit for sailing.

Eating a balanced diet is important for sailors. If you are eating right in general, you will have better concentration, more strength, and be able to build muscles better, which all adds up to sailing better.

No need to go for all the sports-booster supplement foods, either. They are expensive, and if you are eating properly, you'll have the advantage anyway. Save the energy bars for on-the-water instant energy hits.

Eating right means plenty of fresh fruits and vegetables, complex carbohydrates, enough protein—and you know all this, right?

But did you know that if you are exercising and sailing actively, your body actually doesn't want and can't use fat? A well-trained or active body chooses and needs complex carbohydrates to power it up, not a plate of greasy fried chicken or three plates of french fries.

One trick for pepping your body up before a big regatta is to do something called *glycogen-loading.* Most energy stored in the body is found in body fat, but muscles can store some energy in carbohydrate-derived glycogen. If you are going to be racing hard for more than two hours, you can try glycogen-loading, but do it properly.

To try glycogen-loading, starting three days before your regatta, make sure you are getting lots of carbohydrates. Don't wolf down huge meals; eat small portions more frequently. You need to drink plenty of water as you are doing this. Your muscles need to store the water with the glycogen. You may gain a little weight, but it will disappear as you use the glycogen. Reduce your exercising for a couple days before the big regatta, and lay off entirely the day before so your muscles can really soak up the glycogen. For the regatta day, give your stomach a couple hours to digest your meal. Eat sensibly, complex carbohydrates again, but don't overload.

No sugary, fizzy drinks; they may give

you a quick energy boost, but it will be followed by a lull. You need all your energy to last the whole day, so don't go for the short-term burst of sugar, because it almost always comes with a weak, confused follow-up an hour or two later.

During a regatta, especially if you are in a foreign country, don't try the local spicy dish. Wait until the racing is over to expand your culinary experiences. If you're not sure something "agrees" with you, don't take the chance of starting an argument with your stomach; you can't win!

The importance of drinking enough fluids cannot be overemphasized. You will be out on the water, in the sun and wind, and you'll need to replenish your liquid intake frequently.

Try this:

Drink as much as two cups of something (preferably water) two hours before the race.

Have another cup of something (again, water is best) half an hour before you launch.

Try to drink a half to a full cup of something (yep: water again) every half hour during the race.

And treat yourself to another . . . cup of water . . . as soon as you get ashore.

You can drink greatly diluted fruit juice before the race, but remember that it contains sugar, so don't rely just on it. You will learn to *love* water.

Sleeping Right

You may be tempted to forgo sleep for the excitement before a regatta, but you will pay for it on the water the next day. Wait until the racing is over to stay up later than you *know* you should. Your muscles need the rest to perform their best. You have built up a strong body, so don't blow it by getting overtired. There is nothing wrong with crashing early the night before a big race. Check around. All the best sailors value their sleep.

If you are sailing in another time zone, think about resetting your internal clock before you leave home. Just sort of creep up on the idea that things will start either earlier or later than you are used to.

And as soon as you get on the plane, set your watch for the time at your destination, and just accept that as the "Real Time." Sleep on the plane, don't harass the flight attendants.

When you are on the ground, adopt the "when in Rome, do as the Romans do" philosophy. Go to bed at the right local time, even if you think you are too cranked up. Think about your tactics, or plan your Olympic gold medal acceptance speech, but stay in bed.

If you have to get up earlier, just do it. Don't sleep until the last minute and then rush to the first start. Your body will adjust quickly to the new routine.

Coaching Opti Sailing

PART VI

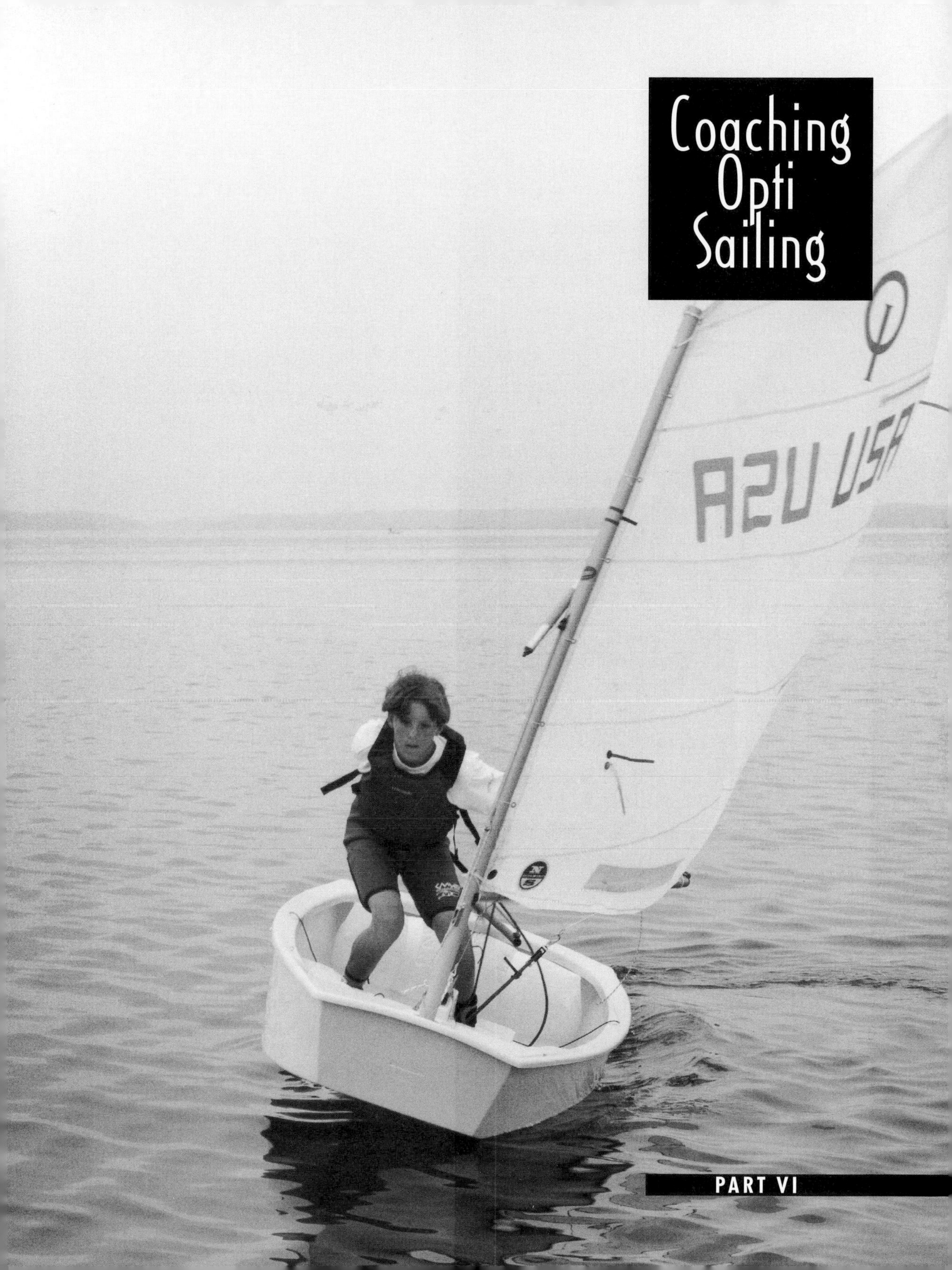

Coaching Young Sailors

Coaching Optimist sailors encompasses a wide range of styles and theories. The limited age range of the Optimist class (eight to fifteen) gives the class a virtually unlimited range of physical and emotional development.

The Optimist is a truly unique boat in that it is very safe and easy for a young child of six to sail, yet complex and tricked out enough to challenge the best fifteen-year-old sailors around the world. There are a great many draws to the Optimist class, including ease of maintenance (even for the eight-year-old), manageable size, and price tag. What keeps kids in the boat after they have learned basic sailing skills is the availability of camaraderie and competition on a local, national, and international basis.

Intense Optimist coaches and overly competitive parents sometimes forget that what makes the camaraderie appealing to the young sailors, and makes the competition worth the work of perfecting their techniques, is the *fun* involved: the fun of sailing, the fun of having the skills to make the boat perform. The challenge for the Optimist coach or parent is to make learning the necessary skills attractive on the young sailor's level.

The Optimist experience is unique in that from their first white fleet regatta, young sailors are competing against sailors as much as eight years older than themselves. No other youth class does this so quickly. For this reason, Optimist sailors have the potential to accelerate the learning process, as well as the potential to become frustrated. A good coach needs to prepare them for this, and help them learn from each experience. This style of competition makes it important for white fleeters to practice with red and blue as much as possible.

Listen carefully to your coach or sailing instructor. You can gain a lot of knowledge in a short period of time from his or her experience.

Coaching on a cold day.

Double-checking flotation gear.

However, it is also important for them to get attention on their own as a beginner group, with appropriate instruction, and for the older sailors to be used to the challenges the younger and lighter sailors can provide.

COACHING BEGINNERS

In the first two years of sailing, the rigors of practice time must be broken up by fun activities in and out of the boat. Pirate days, crazy rig days, scavenger hunts, backwards races, and other activities keep things interesting and allow a variety of class members to shine, yet still center around sailing skills and techniques.

The emphasis on enjoyment and involvement should not preclude necessary repetition of basic sailing skills. Rigging particulars, body position in the boat and on the rail, holding the tiller correctly—all of these can and should become automatic through varied repetition. This is important, as failure to correct sloppy or bad habits only prevents a young sailor from rising to the next level of achievement.

Teaching on the beginner and intermediate level can be difficult. For example, take one of your nonsailing friends and explain the strategy of sailing in an oscillating breeze. Now try to explain it to a child who cannot understand what he or she cannot see. Finding easy, preferably visual, ways to explain sailing and keep it fun is a definite challenge.

COACHING THE OLDER KIDS

Around the age of twelve, as young sailors become more serious, it is often important to take days off the water and use them as team-building experiences. Preteens love this: it gives them time to socialize, to learn about themselves, and to interact with their peers. While Optimist sailing is an individual effort, it is important to take time to emphasize the team aspects of the sport as well. Optimist sailors need teammates to practice, and if one does well, the others on the team can be happy because they all benefit *as* a team.

As the sailors' needs become more demanding, coaching becomes more difficult. Somewhere in blue fleet, their brains are capable of processing more abstract thought while their egos are becoming more sensitive to failure, a tricky combination. A coach must learn, or at least be sensitive to, the needs of each individual and try to supply each with a dose of the appropriate medicine. Sailing affords coaches a particular luxury, in that they can have private, one-on-one meetings with a student by calling him or her over to their boat.

Whether first or last, make it fun.

GOAL SETTING

Goal setting is an important but often overlooked aspect of junior coaching. Learning how to set goals for themselves will carry young sailors through all aspects of life. Of course, everyone wants to win, but in Optimist racing there is only one first-place winner in a fleet that can number two hundred. So why compete? Because there is fun to be had, something new can be learned each time out, and a set of personal or team goals can be met.

It is important to help each sailor determine his or her personal goals, making sure that they are realistic and that the sailor is aware of the stepping-stone, short-term goals along the way. For instance, before she wins the Club Champs, little Susie will have to work on her reaching legs. It is the job of the coach to help Susie identify all the areas where she needs to improve, and to work out a specific plan of improvement for her.

The key to coaching goal setting is to keep a realistic approach. Optimist sailors need to be encouraged to learn, master, and improve their boat-handling and racing skills, but not to the point where they feel driven beyond their capabilities.

Praise for improvement should be sincere but not extravagant. Neither should the sailors sense that they can't possibly live up to expectations.

CRITICIZING AND COMPLIMENTING

Establishing a format for criticizing and complimenting individual and team performances is important for an Optimist coach. As long as the pattern is consistent, and there is a definite system for reviewing performance that allows the sailors to voice their questions, to communicate among their peers and with the coach, hurt feelings can be avoided. Structured land-based prerace meetings, water-based postrace discussions (privately or in groups of two), and land-based postrace general meetings are very important.

Several basic styles of coaching apply to all ages.

Make It Fun

This really is the key. Kids learn faster and better when they are having fun.

Entertain and Intrigue

Keep the sailors wondering, hungry for new information, by presenting it in an entertaining way. This keeps coaches on their toes, too.

Interact

No one likes to be lectured; attention spans for Optimist sailors generally vary from five minutes (age ten) to twenty minutes and more (fourteen and up). Spice up (and break up) lectures with strategically planned questions, demonstrations, and participation.

Modify

If your day's plan seems to be losing your audience's interest, be prepared to switch to something else. Drastically, if necessary.

Keep Stragglers Involved

Haul the daydreamers out of the group to use as "volunteers," maybe as "demonstration boats." Speak to them directly. Ask them questions. Don't drone on. Hop around, be animated, and keep their attention.

Scope Your Audience Out

Pick out the ones who will die of embarrassment if you call on them and involve them more gently. Watch out for the jokers who are just looking to embarrass *you*.

In addition, yours is the task of trying to get the best effort out of each of the sailors, while teaching them increasingly advanced skills and techniques.

If you are coaching serious racers, you need many skills. Because of the disparity of emotional and physical development, you must tailor your programs to the realistic levels of the sailors.

Concern with safety is paramount. Building good sportsmanship should come a close second. Coaching to be an aggressive, winning Optimist sailor cannot take precedence over safety or sportsmanship.

Teaching Format

Teaching and coaching are special arts. Enthusiasm and knowledge of your topic are the key ingredients. We have developed a four-step approach for effective training: *lecture, demonstrate, drill,* and *challenge.*

1. Lecture:

a. Discuss exactly what you plan to do.

b. Explain the theory.

c. Give a pep talk about the reasons that this specific area is important.

d. Illustrate the lecture with specific first-person stories if appropriate.

e. Summarize what is going to happen.

f. Answer questions.

2. Demonstrate:

a. Go through a complete demonstration and repeat it until you are satisfied that everyone in the class understands it.

b. Select students to demonstrate the specific lesson and if there are errors, discuss them *after* the demonstration is completed.

3. Drill:

a. Have the class participate in a drill of the topic. Repetitive drills and constant coaching are the keys to rapid learning.

b. If the drill is not going well, go back to the demonstration stage.

4. Challenge:

Let students demonstrate their new skill by racing or individual testing, but make it fun and challenging.

LECTURES

Read over the material before each lecture so that it is fresh in your mind, and review any tests that you might give so that you will be certain to cover the material in them.

Try to relate your material to specific events that have taken place. Speak directly to your students, look at each of them often. Be friendly and *enthusiastic*. Never assume your students know the material. Take the time to explain every detail. You might explain the reason why a sailor capsized, for example, or discuss a good mark rounding. Answer all the questions your students have, no matter how basic. Ask questions during your lecture to keep the class alert and to stress specific points.

Try to keep the class in one or two rows only. This maintains order and helps keep their attention.

Illustrating ideas on a blackboard or magnetic board is always a big help when lecturing, but be sure that your drawings are neat and clear. Though it is fun to have classes outside, you will find that your students learn more in the more formal atmosphere of a classroom and in front of a blackboard.

Never hesitate to review material. Only a few students may ask questions, and others might be afraid to ask, even though they do not fully understand the material.

Remember that most kids learn visually and physically, so make your pictures clear and do a lot of land drills to explain tough stuff for the water.

DEMONSTRATIONS

Lecturing helps to introduce and organize material, but demonstrations are critical to a student's understanding of the point under discussion. The best results appear to be made when demonstrations are held in small groups—four sailors and one instructor rigging a boat, for example, with each student having the opportunity to rig the boat after the demonstration. We recommend using the Optimist to demonstrate step-by-step maneuvers on land. The following list contains some suggested demonstrations you should set up.

Beginner

1. Point out the different parts of a boat and review.

2. Have the class stand around a sail and discuss its parts.

3. The points of sailing: have the class sit on the dock and watch the instructor in a boat illustrate each point of sailing.

4. Use of a life jacket.

5. How to fold a sail.

6. Rigging a boat.

7. Launching a boat.

8. Capsizing.

9. Landing.

10. Proper boat posture—where to sit, how to trim, hold a hiking stick, hike, move around in a boat.

11. How to get out of the no-go zone.

12. Basic right-of-way rules (using two boats).

13. Knots.

14. Anchoring.

15. Basic racing techniques.

16. Avoiding collisions (Tiller Toward Trouble).

17. Getting into the safety position.

18. Bailing out your boat.

19. Towing.

Advanced

1. Racing posture.

2. Trimming and steering.

3. Acceleration.

4. Tacks, jibes, maneuvering.

5. Sail trim, weight, rudder relationship.

6. Starting techniques.

7. Tactical and rules situations (on the water).

8. Trim and tuning demonstrations on shore.

9. Heavy air sailing: S jibes.

DRILLS

Drills are very helpful when learning to sail and race, as they keep a sailor concentrating on one specific aspect. Each day you can go through several drills. Make sure it doesn't get boring!

Coaching when sailors are going through drills is very important. Again point out one error at a time and be positive (for example: "Everything looks good, but try to keep the boat flatter after a tack").

Drills should be a major part of your sailing curriculum. They are great warm-ups and cool-downs. They also eliminate competitiveness within the group because it's not a race with one winner. Racing should be saved for the end of practice, to shake out what the kids have learned. Be creative with drills; they can be designed to simulate virtually every tactical situation on the water.

The best time to conduct drills is during a time when boats are waiting for others to sail out to a course or back in. Time on the water is valuable, so make the most out of it. Do not wait for all boats to finish. Start giving practice starts as soon as one third have crossed the line. On the way in, have the sailors go through tacks and jibes (see chapter on "Practice").

On-the-Water Coaching Techniques

Approach a boat with your powerboat from behind and to leeward. This cuts down any disturbance from your boat, and it makes it easier for a sailor to hear and see you.

Point one thing out at a time. If there are many mistakes, return later. Let the sailor work out one problem at a time. Return to many boats as often as possible; don't spend a lot of time with one boat. If a boat is having problems, keep coming back until that phase is being executed properly. If there seems to be a universal misunderstanding, bring the class back in and do the lecture, land drill, or demonstration again. Give specific commands. Say "trim the main in to the quarter"—not "trim the main a little."

Send boats on a long enough race or course so you have time to get to every boat. Stay where the action is. Motor near the mark so that you can follow the sailors through the maneuvers. Do not try to watch several sailors at once. Watch each sailor carefully and then give a pointer.

If there is a particular problem, it may help to have one sailor get in the powerboat and watch others, or sit and watch you demonstrate.

Be careful maneuvering around sailboats. Try to keep one hand on the throttle and one on the wheel. If using a loudhailer, maintain a slow speed and do not change course.

COACHING WITH A VIDEO CAMERA

A simple video camera can be a valuable aid to an Opti coach. It is recommended that each coach have his own video camera.

The best way to use the camera is to record while your sailors are racing or running through drills. At the end of the session, watch the tape and you will be able to summarize their good points and their errors. Don't try to coach and video at the same time—just get their boat in the screen and go!

Use a video recorder to help sailors study their technique.

A video camera will also work well if you record the actions of boats on an individual basis. Try to be brief with your comments. Also, it is a good idea to watch the tape first before you show it publicly to save any embarrassment.

Attention spans are short. Video is super-effective for holding Opti sailors' attention. They love to see themselves on tape and generally learn very visually at that age. Video can make a long debrief seem short, holding their attention for as long as an hour.

KEEP A NOTEBOOK

Sailors should be encouraged to keep a written record of their sailing experiences. Good sailors keep track of

149

the races they are in, noting the conditions of the race course, what the wind and tides were doing, and how they did in the weather conditions.

This will help your students identify areas of skill that they have mastered, and areas that they need to practice. They should note any rigging changes they might have made and how the changes affected their sailing.

By keeping a log, your students have notes to refer to the next time they sail in that place, or under those conditions. If they also write down their racing tactics, they will soon be able to see what works.

Because Optimists are sailed all over the world, your students could also be creating a pretty exciting travel diary as well. Have them keep track of friends they meet in other places by writing their names and addresses in their log book, as well as all the important sailing information.

They should collect favorite articles and pictures. It's amazing what you can learn from information that is saved and reread.

Instructor's Safety Review

It is of the utmost importance for sailing instructors to concern themselves with safety throughout the sailing program. No thought or action should be dismissed when considering the safety of your students.

On land we recommend a student/instructor ratio of 12:1. On the water, there should always be two chase boats available for a fleet of fifteen to twenty boats.

WEATHER FORECASTS

Instructors should check the weather forecasts daily. If the forecast calls for bad weather and the sky indicates its approach, no boats should be allowed on the water. Care must also be taken regarding wind velocity. To some extent, the maximum velocity that you should allow boats on the water is dependent on the experience of your students. You should encourage the sailors to try for the next level, but keep in mind their capacities. Don't ever tell them they can't do it, but guide them toward a safe decision they make on their own.

SAFETY BOATS

Powerboats are a must for a safe sailing program. Although one launch or whaler might serve the purpose, two are better and give an added measure of safety. Safety boat skippers should be familiar with and have practiced the procedures for handling capsized boats and towing Optis.

LIFE JACKETS

Each Optimist sailor must properly wear a USCG-approved life jacket and whistle. You should enforce this rule with no exceptions.

SWIMMING

Students entering the class must be able to swim, and instructors should set up tests to ensure this. At a minimum, a sailor should be able to swim one hundred yards and tread water for five minutes. Life jackets are mandatory even for those who pass.

KNOW YOUR STUDENTS

Instructors should get to know their students to help ensure their safety. By knowing them well, instructors can identify those who are apt to disrupt a class or fool around on the water and cause accidents, as well as those who are apt to panic in the event of a capsize. Special efforts can then be made to work with these students, review preventative measures and the steps they should take after a capsize to ensure their safety.

CAPSIZE AND RESCUE PROCEDURES

One of the most important drills of the summer is to have each student go through capsize and rescue practice. In a rescue operation, the first thing the instructor should do is make sure that the sailors are all right. Approach the capsized boat from leeward and try to keep the sailor calm. In areas where the water is cold, or if the sailors seem cold, get them out of the water immediately.

If the boat can be righted, have the sailor free the sheet and bring the boat head-to-wind. Use the centerboard as a lever and pull on it (not the lower part) to right the boat. Have the sailor rest before continuing to sail.

If you are going to tow the boat, unclip the mainsheet from the bridle. If the boat has turned turtle, have the student attempt to turn the boat on its side by standing with toes on the rail and rocking the board toward himself. When the boat is on its side, he must pull the board down until he can grab the rail and climb in. When the boat is righted, the student should begin bailing it out, and when it is adequately dry have the student board from the stern or side and continue the bailing. He should then check the boat to see that nothing has been damaged and that all the equipment is there. (If the mast is stuck in the mud, it is better to anchor the powerboat upwind and throw a line to the boat. Never try to pull a mast out of the mud by using the engine.)

OPTIMIST TOWING PROCEDURE

Towing a group of Optimists is very simple. The class rules indicate that each boat must be fitted with an 8-meter floating painter with a small loop or bowline knot tied in the end. Make sure the painter is tied to the mast step! Sailors should coil this line neatly when not sailing, and tuck it up under the inside lip of the bow.

When light air or safety reasons call for a tow, the sailors should sail up to the safety boat close enough for the instructor to reach in and grab the coiled line. This can be done with the safety boat anchored or under way (going very slowly!).

When the safety boat has the child's bowline, the instructor needs to loop the end around a cleat on the boat. The sailor needs to pull his daggerboard up halfway, unclip his mainsheet from the bridle, and then sit back and steer straight behind the boat in front of him.

When adding another boat to the tow, the instructor simply runs the next boat's painter through the loop at the end of the first boat's painter. This moves the new boat into the first position in the tow. Each additional Opti painter should be passed through the loop of the previous boat. This will form a continuous string of boats carrying only their own weight!

Take care that the painter stays on top of the boat; do not let it get caught underneath or alongside the bow. A small powerboat can easily tow eight to ten Optimists.

To release the tow, the safety boat simply drops the painter of the first boat, and each sailor pulls his own painter in!

Drills to Improve Boat Handling

Being confident and comfortable in a boat on all points of sail is the best way to enjoy sailing, and the surest way to perfect racing performance.

There are any number of drills you can use to help young sailors gain confidence and improve their skills.

TACKING DRILLS

All boats start on starboard tack, and tack on the whistle.

JIBING DRILL

After the tacking drill, a series of whistles indicates that the boats should turn downwind and jibe on every whistle, staying synchronized.

BACKWARDS RACING

Start at the windward mark, and literally sail backward to cross the starting line. Boats keep booms out as far as possible, keep the boat flat, and sit next to the daggerboard trunk. Remember, steering is "backward," too.

MACHINE GUN STARTS

Give a two-minute rolling start. Boats sail for one minute, start again in two (starting gun is also two-minute warning for next start). This also works for one-minute starts.

STOP AND GO

One whistle: stop boat quickly. Two whistles: get sailing again. Great upwind and downwind.

100-YARD BEAT

Use a two-minute start and a really short windward leg. Object is to win the beat.

WATER BALLET

Establish follow-the-leader with less than a boatlength between boats. Leader jibes around to come up behind last boat, creating a circle of boats. One whistle: all change direction to the inside. Two whistles: all change direction to the outside.

MATCH RACE STARTS

Boats go one-on-one for the start, each trying to drive the other away but stay in advantageous position.

LAST BEAT

All boats start in a preset order and race to the finish, trying to improve their positions.

RUDDERLESS RACE

A very short triangle course, sailed with no rudders (weight and sail control only).

RABBIT STARTS

The fleet luffs to leeward of the layline upwind from a mark. One boat ("the rabbit") rounds the mark and trims to close hauled. Each boat must duck the rabbit and head up.

TWO-TACK BEATS

All boats are limited to two tacks to make an entire windward leg.

30-SECOND START

Even after the two-minute sequence has elapsed, the coach may call a five-second countdown to the start after the thirty-second whistle.

Drills to Improve Speed

The best way to improve your speed in an Optimist is to sail enough to get a "feel" for the way your boat is moving through the water. You will soon be able to tell if your boat is moving at its optimum speed.

We recommend sailing against another boat to test speed. When you experiment with adjustments, one boat should make one adjustment at a time.

Practice

Practicing Alone

Practicing alone is easy. You can concentrate on becoming adept at all kinds of maneuvers, and test your boat speed.

Through discipline and desire, sailors can organize their own practice sessions. They can last from one to three hours.

When practicing alone, you have the steadiest of all competitors: *time.* Pick out two channel markers to use as windward-leeward marks. The shorter your course, the better. Race from Buoy A to Buoy B and clock the time it takes. Resail the course, trying to better the time.

There are many drills you can use to improve maneuvers and seamanship. Try to practice them as if the Olympics depended on your performance. Be serious, concentrate, and focus on every move you make in the boat.

SPINNER DRILL

This is a series of two full-circle turns, or what is known as a 720.

Sail in as small a circle as you can, making two revolutions, then reverse and sail in the opposite direction two times. Do this as quickly as possible, trying to keep your speed up the whole time.

To begin a spinner, sail to windward and begin a fast roll tack.

Once your tack is completed, pull the tiller all the way to windward, and let go of it using your body weight and sail trim to turn the boat while dumping the main as quickly as possible.

Keep your boat flat. A heel will give you trouble bearing away.

Do not jibe the sail until the wind is dead astern.

When you do jibe (roll it), get your sail in quickly. This will help you round up into the wind for your next spin.

Keep your spinners up for a series of two turns—you'll just about be dizzy by then—then change direction. Spinners don't take much time; they give you excellent practice and a physical workout, too!

PRACTICE TACKS

Other than bad windshifts and slow speed on a windward leg, the most ground is lost while tacking, so it is important to practice, practice, practice.

When you practice tacks, always do them in sets of six or more, never spending more than a few seconds between each tack.

After each set, spend a minute or two

thinking about the series. What seemed to slow you down?

Are you rolling the boat through the tack properly? Go through your maneuvers and work on balance, mainsheet handling, and getting from one side of the boat to the other with the proper motion.

Remember that accelerating after a tack is important. Your recovery is helped by the roll, so make it work for you. You will probably have to bear off a little to gain speed, but practice making this as small a course change as possible.

In stiff breezes, try not to bear off at all. Either steer a high course after the tack or ease the mainsheet to help keep your boat flat after you have come through the wind.

FIGURE EIGHTS

Find or set two buoys close together, about two boatlengths apart. Start a series of figure eights around these marks. Be sure to clear the line completely between the marks when approaching for the crossover of the figure eight.

WAVES

Everyone needs practice sailing big waves. If a powerboat throws you a hefty wake, take a minute and set up for some surfing practice. Remember to pump your sails (once each wave—make it count), and shift your weight to keep the boat balanced and your speed at its maximum.

RUDDERLESS

Steering without your rudder builds your skill at balancing and adjusting your position in the boat, and your sail-handling abilities. Sit forward on your centerboard trunk and hold the boom like a sailboard boom. You may want to unclip your mainsheet.

BACKWARDS

Practice this skill. It will help you on the starting line and in getting out of the "no-go zone."

Hold your boom out until it catches the wind and your boat starts to move backwards. Remember that your rudder works in reverse now! To starboard, and you go to starboard.

SINGLE BUOY, MULTIPURPOSE

You may use a single buoy as one end of a starting line, the windward mark, reach mark, leeward mark, a reference point for your tacking radius, or as a point to judge the set and drift of the current. Useful!

For starting line practice, sail away from the mark on a broad reach in the opposite direction from that which would take you back to the mark close hauled. Start with two minutes set on your stopwatch. At one minute sail up to the line and practice holding your boat on the buoy for one minute. As you get better, increase the time to two minutes. Make sure that at the end of the time you can bear off and accelerate off the line.

To use the buoy as the windward mark, approach by judging your layline. As you bear off, ease your sail and keep the boat flat. Practice taking the mark both to starboard and to port. Approach on both tacks bearing away, and also bearing away and jibing.

To use the buoy as a reach mark, jibe around it in both directions. Practice your tactics here. Stay wide as you approach, close as you round the mark and harden up.

Remember to have a course figured out for after your mark roundings so you won't stall out by trying for a too-high course, or lose ground by falling off too much.

You will judge whether you are using the turning space around marks properly by watching the mark as you round it. And you will be able to see what the current is doing by comparing the position of the buoy, as you sail up on it, to a fixed spot on the shore or compared to another mark.

Practicing in Pairs

A second boat serves as a benchmark, and the practice improves both boats. Not only can two boats tune up against each other, but they can also set up match races and an organized series of drills and maneuvers.

If you find you are losing most of the exercises, don't be discouraged. Remember that the work you are doing now will add up to help you later with the rest of the fleet, as well as with your practice partner!

And if you are winning, do not get cocky. Be considerate of your partner's feelings and abilities. You want your partner to be sailing his best to help you keep up your skills. Talk over what you might be doing differently. This will help keep your practice partner's interest up, and continue to provide you with a challenge.

To get the most out of these drills, you want to sail as aggressively as you possibly can. If you have developed a good attitude with your practice partner by discussing what works and what doesn't, you both will stay psyched up and enthusiastic. It's no good to be practicing with someone who isn't giving the practice session his best effort. Know the rules, always work to perfect your boat-handling skills, and don't ever give up.

First, set all controls the same on both boats: sprit, vang, boom preventer, mast rake, daggerboard, and mainsheet. It helps if you have similar equipment, especially sails. Everything. You want the two boats to be as equal as possible.

Then just simply sail along with the other boat. Keep clear air, no blanketing, and try to stay in the same force of wind. You are trying to learn here. You can split tacks: sail off on opposite tacks for a timed leg, say two minutes, then tack and see how you cross. This is a good way to determine the favored side of a course before a race!

Adjust one thing each session. See what happens if you adjust your sprit, or your vang, or your mainsheet; put your daggerboard down farther, or pick it up a little. Compare the performance of the two boats with these various changes. Top sailors know their boats, and how they react to every condition.

Try a rabbit start. Boat A dips the stern of Boat B while sailing to windward. Boat B continues on course for two or three boatlengths, then tacks. The time Boat B spent tacking should be the same as the time lost by Boat A when dipping, so both boats will start evenly.

Now work to get your speed up. Sail trim, working the puffs, paying attention to your angle of heel and to your course will all matter here. Steer steadily—you don't want your rudder moving around too much and creating drag. Practice all your upwind skills.

Once one boat develops an obvious lead, start all over again. Be honest with the other boat, and compare notes about any adjustments you might have made.

Tacking duels are good two-boat drills. Start with Boat A crossing the stern of Boat B. Boat A then tacks on Boat B, which then tacks for clear air. Make these tacks as quickly as possible, but always stay in control of your boat, and keep your momentum up. Keep your boat properly balanced. Too much heel can round you up just when you need speed. You don't want to stall in a tacking duel!

Tacking duels are physically demanding but good fun, too. At the same time you are watching your competitor, you also have to be making sure your tacks are as smooth and clean as possible. You want clear air, and you want smooth-as-possible water. Wait a second if there is a sloppy chop. It'll pay off. Downwind, practice jibing ten times, seeing which boat can complete the series in the shortest time, covering the most distance.

Practicing in pairs also can help expand your good sailing attitude. It's always better to practice against someone you think might be better than you. As in all sports, this only improves your game.

Practicing in a Fleet

Practicing with a fleet of boats takes greater organization than practicing alone or in pairs, but these practice sessions can take several forms. You can use a regatta as a practice or a tune-up for a more important regatta, or you can participate in one of a number of clinics or seminars.

Organized practice sessions help sailors concentrate on specific techniques they might not normally use during a race. Clinics work best if there is a leader or an instructor to set the pace. But the leader can be one of the competitors in your fleet. For example, if there are ten boats in your racing fleet, perhaps one boat can sit out, and each participant can rotate as the leader of the clinic.

Let regattas be your final examination. While at a practice session, do not be concerned with being first over the line; instead, be more concerned with working on specific techniques, such as starts, boat handling, mark roundings, and boat speed. If someone is watching and helping you from outside your boat, you will probably learn quickly and with greater ease.

The typical training day might include speed testing, boat-handling exercises, and short-course races. An entire clinic can be run in just one afternoon or evening. The trick is to concentrate on one thing at a time. All sailors are winners when they participate in training sessions.

The traditional way to train is to put it all together at a regatta, but this really is a hit-or-miss method. With an organized practice session you learn things much sooner and you bring up the overall level of all sailors because everyone at the session is working on a single technique. Collective wisdom speeds the learning process.

STARTING DRILLS

There are a number of starting drills that can be practiced, including:

Slow Start

From thirty seconds before the start until ten seconds before it, all sails must be completely luffing. This teaches boat control on crowded lines when you have to get into the "first row" early, hold your position, and accelerate fast.

Speed Start

From thirty seconds until the start, you must sail at full speed on a close-hauled course with sails trimmed optimally. No luffing of sails or bearing away is allowed.

Port Approach Start

From one minute to thirty seconds you must be on port tack—then you are free to go back to starboard whenever you want.

Starting with No Watch

This forces the sailor to concentrate on his technique and keep careful time of his own start. The instructor can give signals at thirty-second intervals and eventually expand it to one-minute and finally two-minute intervals and make the sailor start at his own time.

Automatic Recall

On every start two boats are automatically recalled and have to round the ends regardless of whether they were over or not.

Downwind Starts

Race downwind to a leeward mark,

which forces crowded leeward mark rounding.

UPWIND DRILLS

Once the fleet has started and is sailing upwind, there are a number of ways to practice boat-handling techniques and tactics on a beat.

Cone Drill

The fleet starts normally, but after the start they are confined to a triangle formed by the two ends of the line and the session leader in a motorboat traveling straight upwind. When a sailboat reaches the imaginary wall of the triangle, it must treat this as an obstruction and tack. The leader tries to hail those boats that go beyond the cone walls. This drill focuses on tacking skills, the mechanics of ducking a starboard tacker, and the use of Rule 43 ("Close-hauled, Hailing for Room to Tack at Obstructions"). The fleet really bunches up as they get farther away from the line and the triangle gets smaller, so the drill must be abandoned before it gets ridiculous.

Tacking Drill

All boats start normally and remain on starboard tack until a signal (usually preceded by a short countdown for warning) comes from the motorboat upwind of the fleet. At that point, all boats must tack. After several minutes of this drill, it will become obvious which boats are tacking well, and they can be asked to demonstrate their techniques for the fleet.

Acceleration Drill

This is a variation on the tacking drill in which all boats completely luff their sails on starboard tack until they stop. On a signal, all boats trim to accelerate. This is a good way to learn the proper steering, weight placement, and sail control for whenever you're going at less than full speed.

Helm Control

All boats sail the same tack and make adjustments to their trim (sail, rig, etc.) one at a time on command to determine how each change affects the boat's "helm" and speed.

360 Degrees

Again the boats sail upwind on the same tack, and at the whistle each must do a complete 360-degree turn (or two turns of 720 degrees). This is great for improving execution of turns and 720-degree penalties.

DOWNWIND DRILLS

After sailing upwind for about three to five minutes, you can use downwind drills to have the fleet end up at the starting line. If the fleet is too scattered, it is time to regroup and start another drill on a line. The trick is to use all available time concentrating on sailing.

Jibing Drill

All boats bear off to a broad reach (or beam reach or run) on the same tack and jibe on the signal. It's important for the motorboat to remain upwind of the fleet and repeat the instructions before each signal to ensure that everyone understands what is coming next.

RACES

Restricted Tacks Race

Only two or four tacks are allowed on the beat. This puts a premium on having clear air at the start and judging layline.

Multiple Tacks Race

In this drill there is a required number of tacks (ten, for example) that must be made between the start and the first mark. This rewards good tacking, with very little emphasis on boat speed. Offwind you could require a given number of jibes as well.

Team Racing

This is one of the best ways to practice your racing ability and is great for teaching how to control other boats. It is also fun to be a part of a team effort on the course.

Match Racing

Split the fleet into pairs and give a separate start for each. You can start two races at once by setting the committee boat in the middle of two buoys. This practice is excellent for one-on-one tactical situations and also for straight-line speed development.

FUN DRILLS

It works well to keep things lively by mixing the more "serious" drills with a few creative and fun ones. If you do it right, these can also help develop specific skills while being fun to do.

Backwards Sailing

On a signal, all boats must start sailing backwards. This is good for developing boat-handling control and sail control, but sometimes it not as easy as it seems.

No Rudder

Have everyone take out their rudders and try to start sailing on a starboard-tack reach. It is helpful to pull the centerboard up halfway or so to keep the center of lateral resistance aft. This drill is excellent for teaching sailors how to steer using sails and weight. Once the participants have mastered this, have them sail at other angles to the wind and do tacks or jibes.

Serpentine

This is basic follow-the-leader, and it can lead to some spectacular water ballet with a well-choreographed group. The key is to begin the serpentine with the leader sailing on a beam reach back and forth until all the fleet falls in line. Then the creativity can begin.

Standing Race

Sailors must stand while skippering their boats; this teaches coordination with weight.

PART VII

For Parents Only

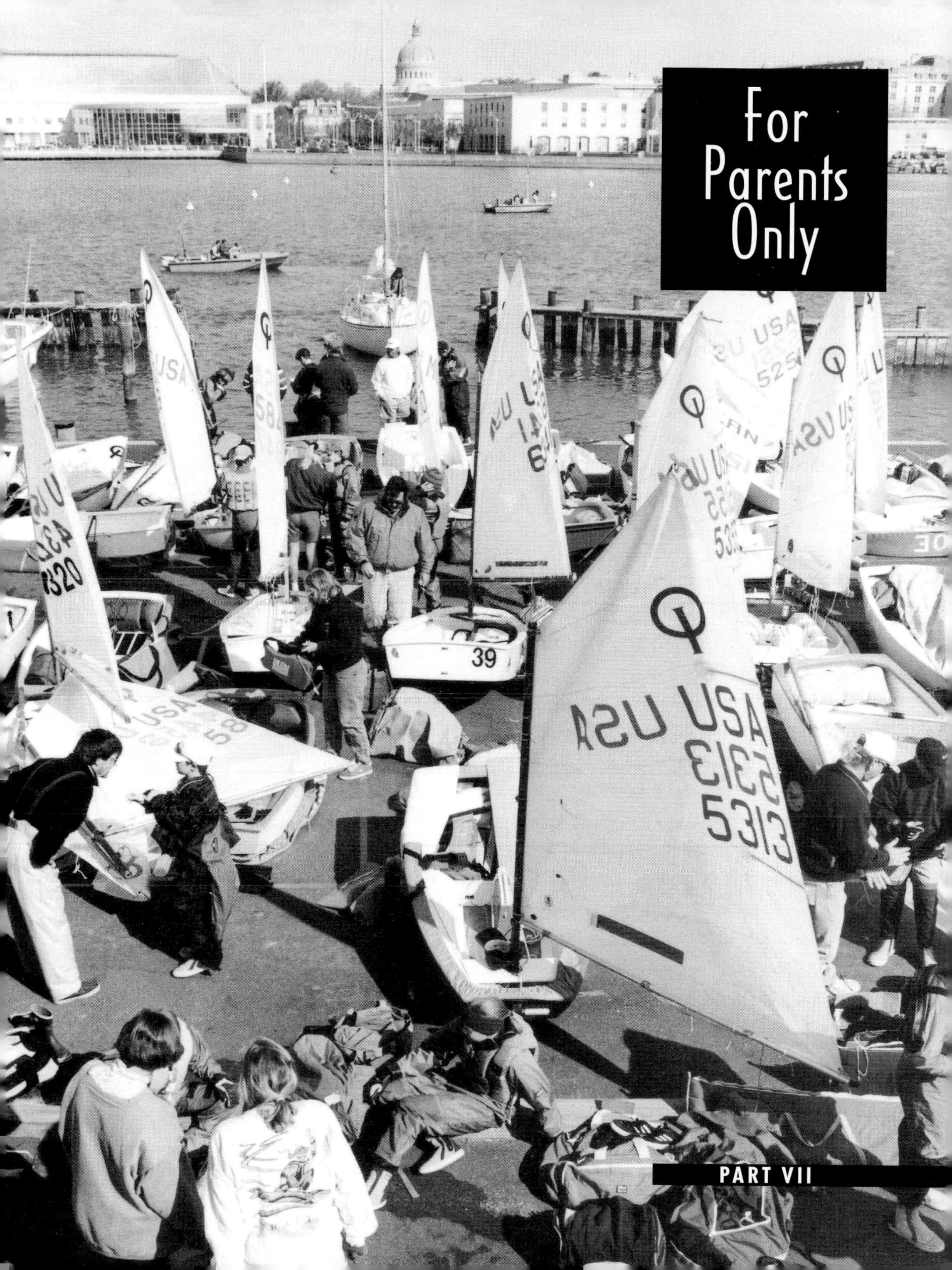

OptiMania: A Note for Parents

by Gary Jobson

OptiMania is sweeping America. Our young sailors are learning to sail and race in this tiny, challenging dinghy in record numbers. The quality of sailing instruction has improved dramatically, thanks to standardized teaching methods and common boats. Conformity allows for measurable progress. But when comparisons are made there is pressure to excel. Many young sailors are being pushed hard. Sometimes too hard. For parents and instructors it is essential to carefully balance providing sailing opportunity and "overcoaching." If you put too much pressure on kids, burnout or rejection can easily replace enthusiasm for learning.

Look at the example often found in Little League baseball, where parents sometimes try to relive their own early days vicariously through their children. It is disastrous to push kids faster than their own pace. Nudging children into sailing, I have found, is a fascinating challenge, and it must be done with care to preserve the children's enthusiasm and excitement.

At a recent Opti regatta in Annapolis, 104 boats competed. I counted 63 coach boats following the fleet. Around the docks you could sense the pressure many of the young sailors were under.

I only had to look as far as my own family. Our oldest daughter, Kristi, first took Optimist dinghy sailing lessons at the San Diego Yacht Club at age seven. Looking back, it was a mistake on my part to start her so young. Because her dad was an active sailor, Kristi perceived that everyone instantly expected her to excel. Within two years, Opti sailing gave way to a variety of worthy activities. But sadly, for me at least, sailing was not one of them.

Hoping to learn from experience, I took Kristi's younger twin sisters, Ashleigh and Brooke, day-sailing occasionally on a twenty-eight-foot Herreshoff sloop, and we spent a few weeks each summer cruising on a schooner. But there was no talk of Opti sailing, let alone racing.

To understand how kids feel, think back to your earliest days. My fears included heeling, capsizing, and getting stuck in irons. It is hard to overcome early fright, so one must be patient.

The best way to lead is by example. Your attitude has a major impact on impressionable minds. It helps when sailing is not an end in itself. Small doses (one or two hours at a time) are better than long days on the water. Include lots of activities around the boat. I find that kids, like adults, enjoy sailing best when given a purposeful job. Steering with as little coaching as possible, for example, should be used as a major reward.

Go easy when introducing racing. Explain that the difference between winning and losing is not that important. The true priority should be on learning. It helps to demonstrate that most champions experience many defeats before finally achieving success.

For young sailors, expert coaching can be helpful. I think it is better for an outside instructor to work with children rather than a parent.

In competition, sailors need guidance and encouragement. The best way to coach is often by asking questions after a race or a practice session. Learning should be fun. Making one point at a time is better in the long term.

Deemphasize over-exultation when winning. The trendy antics of many professional football players after every play are a disgraceful example. Teach young sailors to show respect for their competitors. Many of your most valuable lessons are learned by talking with your rivals. North Sails president Tom Whidden and I have spent many years racing against each other on different boats, but we always find time to compare notes after a regatta. In the long term, we both are stronger.

The desire to learn and compete must come from within. So providing the reasons to learn should be your underlying goal. Show kids what their future can be in sailing. Let them sail boats of all sizes. Get kids involved in decision making. Don't always race. Kids love games. Let older junior sailors set the pace.

To help encourage Ashleigh and Brooke to sail, I recruited a young, enthusiastic instructor, Tucker Thompson, to give a three-hour "fun" lesson. Thanks to Tucker, and to my pleasant surprise, both Ashleigh and Brooke *asked* to join our (Annapolis) yacht club junior program.

For me, it will take discipline to let them set their own pace. But good things may happen. Even the Olympic organizers have recognized that pressures on thirteen-year-old gymnasts can have a negative effect: in the future, Olympians will have to be sixteen to compete.

In sailing, ages vary as to the best time to get kids on the water by themselves. For Kristi, seven was too early. For the twins, nine was about right. And for me, as a parent, patience pays.

Tips for Parents: Preparing for Opti Regattas

• Housing can be arranged at most "away" regattas, and the name of a housing contact will be listed on the information sheet for the regatta. In most cases, the families who provide housing will have an Opti sailor of their own, and you and your child will have a good opportunity to make new friends and learn more about Opti sailing from your hosts. The best visiting families think ahead and bring a gift for the hostess (a fruit basket or some gourmet goodies perhaps) as well as perhaps a breakfast treat for everyone (a selection of bagels, for example). If you can reach the host in advance, it's wise to ask if you should bring sleeping bags or pillows or linens. Host families usually provide a basic breakfast, but for other meals you should consider yourself on your own. (Lunch and sometimes dinner are often served at the regatta location.) Be a good guest and try to disrupt the host family's life as little as possible. Offer to strip the beds when you leave, and don't forget a thank-you note.

• Whether the regatta is at home or away, don't forget to bring extra supplies. While some regattas will have supplies sold on the premises, many will not. A few basic extras include an extra paddle, an extra wind direction signal (if your child uses one), extra sail ties, and any other equipment that your child relies upon and might misplace.

• Bring something to amuse your child in the event of bad weather. Often the sailors will keep themselves busy, but sometimes a full day of rain at a strange yacht club can last forever, and a book or a hand-held video game or a deck of cards can come in very handy.

• Sailors should always bring a water bottle out on their boat when they race. It's a good idea to freeze a few water bottles the night before a race. Frozen bottles can be tucked into the Opti and will usually be cool and refreshing when the thirsty sailor reaches for one.

• Don't forget snacks. Most yacht clubs have snack bars or nearby delis, but some are fairly isolated. If your child doesn't like the lunch served at the regatta, it will be important to have some fruit or crackers or granola bars to hold her till dinner.

• Pack lots of dry clothes, especially if you are traveling.

• A few large plastic garbage bags for wet clothes and equipment come in handy.

• Don't forget to pack an indelible pen for labeling any equipment or clothing you acquire.

• A few Ziploc plastic bags are useful for stowing snacks that your sailor will take out onto the race course. They are also crucial for holding a copy of the course (which the sailors will be given before the race).

• A roll of duct tape is always useful. You can duct-tape the copy of the race course (in its Ziploc bag) on the inside wall of the hull of the Opti so your sailor can refer to it while sailing. Many last-minute repairs can be achieved with duct tape.

• Finally, do anything you can to reduce tension. Most children are quite nervous before any race. Parents can get frantic in the course of preparing for the day, and kids pick up on that anxiety. Try to be calm and relaxed and encouraging. Remember, this is supposed to be fun!

The
Eternal
Optimist

PART VIII

The Eternal Optimist

As you grow older and you master Optimist dinghy sailing, your goals and aspirations will include other types of sailing. Deciding what boat to sail is easy once you have set your goal.

Look for a boat or type of racing that is competitive. We like to primarily race in one type of boat and then vary the routine in a larger and a smaller boat. Racing in a larger boat helps you develop teamwork, while smaller boats keep you in tune with the wind, the water, and boat handling.

There is no limit to what you can achieve in sailing. The following is an overview of different styles you may choose.

CLASSES

Sailboat classes come in all shapes and sizes. It is important to select a boat that you will be able to sail competitively for your size. We recommend sailing an international class with a good organization. It helps if this class is sailed near your home. Look for a class that has a lot of good competition and top sailors who are willing to help newcomers.

List of Recommended Classes

Singlehanded

Laser	Europe Dinghy
Laser Radial	Finn
Sunfish	Zuma
The Escape	Sailboard
The Topper	Byte

Doublehanded Boats

420	Albacore
Laser 2	Blue Jay
470	Comet
Flying Junior	Fireball
505	Ideal 18
Tornado	International 14
Snipe	Vanguard 15
Star	JY-15
49er	Penguin

Three or More People

Thistle	Melges 24
Lightning	E Scow
Soling	Flying Scot
Etchells	Sonar
J/22	Ultimate 20
J/24	J/80
Mumm 30	Melges 30
Catalina 22	Cal 20
Catalina 27	Aussie 18 Skiff

HANDICAP RACING/ ONE-DESIGN OFFSHORE

Most handicap racing takes place in larger boats with crews of four or more. There are a number of different handicap rules being used. The difference from one-design class racing is that each boat, in handicap racing, is given a time allowance, depending on its measurement. Sailboats go around the course at different speeds, so it is important to keep track of your time.

Boats perform differently in a variety of wind conditions. So handicapping is often difficult. There are many one-design big-boat classes that combine the benefits of level racing with the fun of sailing larger boats.

SCHOLASTIC SAILING

Over 190 scholastic teams are competing in the United States. Racing at the high-school level has increased dramatically over the past ten years. These programs allow many young sailors to compete year-round. Many of America's best collegiate sailors first competed at the scholastic level.

COLLEGIATE SAILING

Each year the Intercollegiate Yacht Racing Association names an All-America Team. Many of America's best sailors are members of the Collegiate Hall of Fame.

Over 250 colleges have active sailing clubs or teams. Many of these teams are varsity sports and have full-time coaches. We believe collegiate sailing is the most competitive sailing available today. You must sail identical boats and rotate every race. It is here that the skill of the sailor is tested to the fullest.

When applying to either a school or a college, find out about their sailing program. Once enrolled, join the team and participate. It may take a while to break into the starting lineup, but once you do, your skills will improve dramatically.

THE OLYMPICS

In sports today the Olympic Games are frequently viewed as the ultimate competition. At present there are ten different sailing classes in the Olympic Games. The best sailors around the world compete to represent their respective companies. To learn how you can become a member of the U.S. Sailing Team, we recommend writing to:

US Sailing
15 Maritime Drive
P.O. Box 1260
Portsmouth, RI 02871

THE AMERICA'S CUP AND MATCH RACING

Begun in 1851, the America's Cup is the world's oldest continually held sporting competition. Today the America's Cup is a match race between two boats held every two to four years. To race in the America's Cup is the ultimate dream of many sailors. The style of competition is match racing, two boats competing against each other. When the boats are even in speed, there is a premium on tactics and boat handling.

But the America's Cup is also a

competition of design and technology. The selected boats are built to a development rule. Over the history of the America's Cup, one of the boats has usually proved faster than the other. For the past thirty years, there have been many teams challenging the defending club. The challengers have actually had the advantage and have won three of the last five Cups.

To get on an America's Cup team you must first have considerable skill in small boats. Then you must learn to work with a crew on a larger boat. It helps to do a lot of ocean racing. Finally, you will need to spend a lot of time on the match-race circuit to fine-tune your match-racing prowess. The best way to get aboard an America's Cup boat is to compete against a skipper in the America's Cup and help that skipper win races.

Many skippers earned their berth by competing in the international match-racing circuit. For many this is a professional activity now attracting television coverage and offering prize money.

In 1992 the Olympic Games included a match-racing discipline. Match racing is best when the two boats are even in speed.

TEAM RACING

Team racing usually pits three or four boats against another team of the same number of boats. There are many variations in scoring. Team racing is very popular at the college level. The premium is on quick thinking and strategy.

DAY SAILING

Many of your most beautiful moments can be spent on the water simply day sailing. There is none of the pressure you experience in racing or practicing, just simply time for you, your boat, and the water. Small boats are special because they keep you close to the water, and you exist as one with the wind and the sea.

Day sailing can take place in a very short period of time and provide tremendous enjoyment and relaxation.

CRUISING

Cruising is a special part of the sport that many people enjoy as they grow older. Many families enjoy cruising on larger boats for extended periods of time.

Cruising can take you to the most remote regions of the world. At every stop spend time exploring, hiking, and taking advantage of shore-side activities.

Although cruising is far different from racing, you will learn when cruising that getting there is all the fun.

Glossary

DIRECTIONS

Starboard	Right side
Port	Left side
Bow (as in *Wow!*)	Front of boat
Stern	Back of boat
Astern	Behind the boat
Beam	Widest part of boat (side)
Windward	Side toward or facing the wind
Leeward	Side away from the wind
Forward or fore	Toward the bow
Aft or after	Toward the stern

WAYS YOU CAN SAIL

Tack	Turn bow through the wind
Jibe	Turn stern through the wind
Close hauled	Sailing as close to where the wind is coming from as possible
Run	Sail with wind almost directly astern
Reaching	Point of sail not close hauled or running
Close reach	Wind slightly ahead of beam
Beam reach	Wind across beam
Broad reach	Wind slightly behind beam

WAYS YOU CAN'T SAIL

In irons	Directly into the wind, sails luffing, no power, can't turn boat with rudder (no go zone)
Capsize	To turn boat on its side in the water
Swamped	Boat is full of water, you need to . . .
Bail	. . . Get water out of the hull

BOAT PARTS

Hull	The boat itself
Gunwales (say "gunnels")	Top edges of the hull's sides
Transom	Flat back end of hull
Thwart	Flat structural piece that goes from one side to the other side of the hull
Mast thwart	Flat structural piece with hole to accept mast
Mast step	Metal fitting that holds bottom of mast in place
Hiking straps	Bands you hook your feet under so you can lean farther out of the boat to maintain balance
Bulkhead	Low wall running from side to side
Flotation	Compartments/inflatable bags that keep boat floating, even turned over

BLADES

Rudder	Attached by pintles and gudgeons to transom, hangs into the water, steers the boat
Tiller	Extends from rudder into the boat and lets you control rudder
Tiller extension (hiking stick)	Lets you control rudder from farther away
Daggerboard	Extends through boat into water, helps keep boat from slipping sideways
Daggerboard well	Holds daggerboard

SPARS

Mast	Holds sail up
Sprit	Holds sail out at the top
Boom	Holds sail out at the bottom
Boom jaws	U-shaped attachment on boom that fits around mast

SAIL

Mainsail	The only sail on an Opti
Grommets	Metal-ringed holes along edges of sail for sail ties
Battens	Stiffeners for the edges of the sail
Batten pockets	Places to put battens in sail
Luff	The edge of the sail along the mast
Foot	The edge of the sail along the boom
Leech	The edge of the sail away from the mast
Head	The top of the sail at the mast
Peak	The top of the sail at the sprit
Tack	Where the sail meets mast and boom
Clew	Where the sail meets end of boom

LINES

Mainsheet	Lets you pull in or let out the sail
Outhaul	Lets you tighten or loosen the sail along the boom
Sail ties	What you use to attach the sail to the boom and the mast
Mast ties	Makes sure mast stays in mast thwart
Sprit tackle	Lets you raise or lower the sprit
Vang	Keeps boom down
Painter	Tie-up or tow line attached to bow
Telltales	Light lines attached to sail to help judge wind direction
Wind pennant	Fits atop the mast, another wind direction helper

SAFETY EQUIPMENT

Bailers	One, better two, lightweight but strong plastic jugs for getting water out of the boat
Life jacket	You wear one *at all times*
Whistle	Attached to life jacket, to call for attention

Acknowledgments

The key to writing a new book is the assistance of dedicated people. In the preparation of *The Winner's Guide to Optimist Sailing* there are a number of people to whom we are grateful for their assistance:

Kip Requardt compiled much of the research for this book. She is an avid sailor, with a deep appreciation for the skills and values Optimist sailors learn.

Amy Gross added many valuable ideas.

Joni Palmer, executive director of the U.S. Optimist Dinghy Class, helped with our quality and consistency, keeping young sailors in mind at all times.

Thanks to Brad Dellenbaugh for his outstanding illustrations. Also to Dan Nerney, who showed remarkable patience taking endless photographs.

Junior sailing instructor Tucker Thompson offered many clever ideas on how to connect with young people.

Thanks also to: Helen Mary Wilkes, International Optimist Dinghy Association, for her help with our historical research; Peter Johnstone, president of Sunfish Laser, for his help and guidance; Kathy Thompson, who spent many long hours in Annapolis bringing all the material presented from the above list together.

And a special thanks to Simon & Schuster senior editor Fred Hills, for his patience and guidance.

We also appreciate the following young sailors for their help taking the photographs:

Brian Baranaskas
Erik Baranaskas
Amanda Clark
Katie Storck
Kinloch Yellott

Index

Numbers in **bold** refer to pages with photos or illustrations.